To Larry Brown,
With best Wishes,

3-24-99

JACKET AND ILLUSTRATIONS DESIGN by Deborah Eftimiades

Chinese Intelligence Operations

Nicholas Eftimiades

Newcomb Publishers, Inc.
Arlington, Virginia 22203-1510

First published by the Naval Institute Press, Annapolis, Maryland 1994

Library of Congress Cataloging Card Number 98-66788

Newcomb Publishers, Inc.
4812 Fairfax Drive
Arlington, VA 22203-1510

Printed in the United States of America by Newcomb Publishers

Reprinted as a paperback, revised.

The views expressed in this study are those of the author and should not be
construed as representing positions of the Department of Defense or the
U.S. Government.

ISBN 0-9649531-2-9

In memory of Dr. George S. Eftimiades,
who taught me about freedom and hard work,
and Harold C. Hilton, Ph.D. George Washington University,
who inspired me to be a sinologist

Contents

Foreword

Confucius, the moralist and teacher of unsurpassed influence in China for millennia, said, "Confronting a foreign invasion, one should resort to deception, which may suffice in repelling the enemy." Yet when his Western counterpart Socrates advocates wile and guile in the name of national security, we are not sure how to respond. This professed emphasis on covert operations—unfettered, to Western eyes, by any ethical constraints—is distinctly Chinese, with deep historical roots. In Chinese statecraft the use of spies is not incompatible with higher principles. Indeed, in his Art of War Sun Tzu gives top priority to the employment of espionage for humanitarian reasons, among others: in war, lack of the "foreknowledge" supplied by secret agents would "entail heavy loss on the people." In light of China's past one begins to understand the relentless endeavors of the PRC government in pursuing its intelligence objectives, aided by a vast network of chameleonic agents abroad and penetrative bureaucracies at home. Chinese government and society construe the notion of intelligence in the broadest possible sense.

Nicholas Eftimiades's remarkable sensitivity to China's strategic tradition sets his book apart from its competitors in this rapidly expanding field. Adroitly avoiding the pitfall of mirror-imaging, he provides a nuanced, systematic, and in-depth examination of the extensive modern-day Chinese intelligence machine and discusses a wide range of policy-related issues of rising importance. The tone of the book reflects not only insight into the past but also a keen awareness of the present and the future. Eftimiades has actively explored valuable sources newly made available by the increasing permeability of Chinese society, enabling him to assess the strengths and weaknesses of China's intelligence services beyond the confines of conventional wisdom. In addition, a delightful writing style unexpectedly accompanies the thoroughness of a rigorous analyst and the serious nature of the topic. Combining his academic background as a sinologist and his professional training as an intelligence officer, Eftimiades makes a unique contribution to the study of intelligence services and of the current state of the People's Republic of China.

Chong-Pin Lin
resident scholar, AMERICAN ENTERPRISE INSTITUTE

Acknowledgments

This book is the product of three years of interviews, documentary research, and analysis. Many people assisted me during those years, and in this short space I can not possibly acknowledge them all. Please indulge me as I present my most profound thanks to all those who answered my routine pleas for help.

Special thanks to Mike Deckert, who raised my computer from the dead and kept it running—friends don't come any better than Mike. In reviewing this work Lee Livingston, Monty Slocomb, and Hayden Peake proved that that which does not kill us makes us stronger. Lee, Charles Luker, and Col. Pat Niemann, USA (ret.), defended my academic integrity and exemplified the meaning of loyalty when jealous bureaucrats failed to understand how an intelligence analyst could think, read, and write outside the work environment.

Thanks to all the scholars who encouraged me to write this work and who supported me in the process. Portions of this book first appeared in Occasional Papers and Reprints in Contemporary Asian Studies, no. 2 (1992), published by the University of Maryland School of Law. Interviews conducted by Michael Swaine, Ph.D., and the International Campaign for Tibet were invaluable sources of information. Also, my most sincere appreciation goes to those Chinese intelligence officers, diplomats, dissidents, and other sources who spent time with me and provided information literally at their own risk.

Acknowledgments would be incomplete without recognizing Richard W. Marsh, Jr., who spent hundreds of hours wading through documents and who conducted a number of interviews in support of this work. His research talents and fortitude are truly exceptional.

Also, I must thank my loving wife Deborah for designing the book cover and illustrations on short notice. Deborah and our children Stephanie, Sophia, Demetra, Tessa, and Theodore had a profound effect on this book. Without their love, affection, constant attention, and Theo's inability to distinguish day from night, I would have been done a year earlier.

Glossary

Accommodation address	An address in another country used to facilitate letters between agents or illegal operatives and foreign governments
Agent	A foreign national recruited for operational purposes
Case officer	An individual who recruits and handles espionage agents
CMC	Central Military Commission of the Central Committee
Co-optee	An official or visitor tasked to conduct a specific activity such as spotting potential recruits or servicing dead drops
COSTIND	Commission of Science, Technology, and Industry for National Defense
Courier	Member of an intelligence organization who carries and delivers messages, information, and instructions to other members
CPC	Chinese Communist party
Cutout	Use of a third party for communication

	between two entities in order to conceal the identity of one
Dead drop	An agreed-upon place where messages are left by agents for case officers and vice versa
GPD	General Political Department of the People's Liberation Army
GSD	General Staff Department of the People's Liberation Army
Handler	See case officer
Handling	The process of clandestinely directing the actions of an agent
HUMINT	Human-source intelligence
Illegal	A trained intelligence officer, often with a false identity, who maintains no overt contact with his or her government
IMINT	Imagery intelligence, derived from collection and analysis of photographs and images from radar and infrared sensors
Intelligence	Raw information that has been compiled and analyzed; informally, data acquired covertly from a classified source
Intelligence officer	See case officer
IO	Information Objective
Legal	Intelligence officer under diplomatic cover, usually working out of an embassy or consulate
MFA	Ministry of Foreign Affairs

MID   Military Intelligence Department

MPS   Ministry of Public Security

MR   Military region

MSS   Ministry of State Security

OPSEC   Operations security

PLA   People's Liberation Army

PLLC   Political Legal Leading Committee

PRC   People's Republic of China

Recruited asset See agent

Recruitment pitch   Offer made by a case officer to a prospec-
                             tive agent

SIGINT   Signals intelligence, gathered from col-
                             lection and analysis of communications,
                             telemetry, and electronic emanations

Source   See agent

TAR   Tibet Autonomous Region

Tradecraft   Espionage methodology

Chinese Intelligence Operations

Part One Introduction

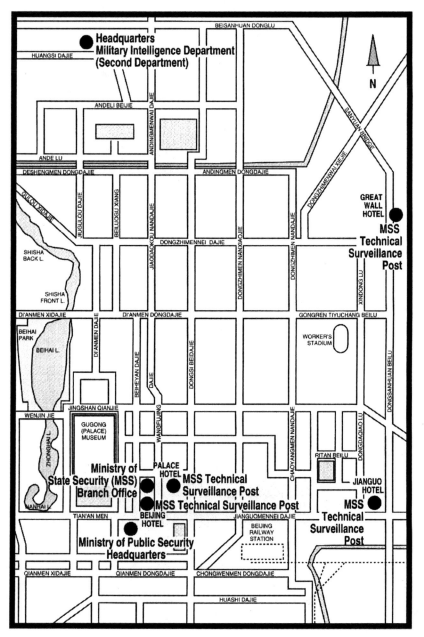

Locations of intelligence facilities in Beijing.

Chapter 1

China's Use of Intelligence

C hinese intelligence operations and methods are relatively new to the Western world. They are not, however, new in themselves. The practice of espionage in China dates back to at least the fifth century B.C., when the proper employment of spies was detailed in a military manual, *Sun Tzu Bing Fa* (Sun Tzu's Art of War). Since that time, The Art of War has been revered as a classic work on the fundamentals of military tactics and strategy. Sun Tzu put a high value on accurate and timely intelligence in daily affairs of state and in support of military campaigns. He attributed a commander's foreknowledge to the proper employment of espionage agents, saying that "no one in the armed forces is treated as familiarly as spies and no one is given rewards as rich as those given to spies."[1]

Sun Tzu was not alone in his appreciation of accurate and timely intelligence in support of diplomatic and military campaigns. China's military history is replete with examples of using espionage to attain policy and military objectives. In the book Chinese Ways in Warfare, Frank A. Kierman, Jr., describes ancient Chinese battle narratives such as the *Tso-Chuan* (Tradition of Tso) of the Eastern Chou period (ca. 770-403 B.C.) and the Shih Chi, an account of Chinese history up to the first century B.C. These narratives are divided into a sequence of preparatory and operational phases, and among the preparatory phases is the collection and analysis of military and relevant diplomatic intelligence information.

It is interesting to note that even in ancient times China had developed and documented an understanding of intelligence needs and practices for military and diplomatic activities. At that time, information requirements were relatively simple: enemy unit size, weaponry, location, and morale; biographical information on enemy commanders; terrain features; and the intentions of neutral and allied forces. In addition, the Tso-Chuan describes intelligence operations employed not only to collect information but also to deceive the opposition and deny them militarily significant information.[2]

Today the People's Republic of China's intelligence needs are far more numerous and complicated than those of ancient times. Yet today's policymakers show the same appreciation for the value of foreknowledge and the proper application of espionage activities in support of the affairs of state. The PRC's intelligence apparatus is more than just a support department for policymakers. It is inextricably linked to the foreign policy decision-making process and internal methods of economic development and political control.

For centuries intelligence services have served their constituents by collecting information about friends and adversaries alike. Indeed, the history of the practice of intelligence operations is ancient and rich. Espionage has been described by insiders as "the world's second oldest profession." To comprehend the structure, roles, and nature of China's intelligence system it is first necessary to understand that such activities do not just happen by themselves. That is, intelligence activities are tied to a government's decision-making processes. Just like diplomatic or military campaigns, intelligence operations in the modern world require careful planning, command and control, communication, and tremendous financial resources. These elements must be organized in some way to accomplish their respective tasks.

Intelligence agencies worldwide share the same overall goal: to provide accurate and timely intelligence to their consumers. To do so they collect raw information from a variety of human and technical sources. They must then collate and analyze that data to separate fact from fiction and make judgments about a variety of past, current, and future events. The completed analytical product, intelligence, is then disseminated to the consumer, whose information requirement started the process. That person or group is then in a position to ask for additional analysis or to implement policy based on the intelligence received. The entire process is known as the intelligence cycle (see fig. 1).

Current world events show no indications of a decrease in the use of espionage to support national policy objectives. Even after the dissolution of the Warsaw Pact, the disintegration of the Soviet Union, and the subsequent reduction in bipolar tensions, intelligence services remain active – and in some cases their level of operations has increased. Global or regional changes in political, military, and economic con-

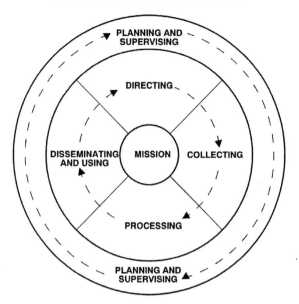

figure 1 "The Intelligence Cycle"

ditions do not diminish the need for accurate intelligence. On the contrary, a nation's need for accurate and timely intelligence corresponds to the level of global or regional instability and the scope of its interests worldwide.

From the end of World War II until recently the Soviet Union and its allies were considered the primary military threat to the United States' global interests. As a result, American intelligence and counterintelligence agencies gave a great deal of attention to the espionage capabilities of the Warsaw Pact nations. Considerably less effort was dedicated to identifying and neutralizing the espionage activities of nations such as China that presented no comparable military threat. Although it has the largest armed forces in the world, the PRC has never developed (and is not likely to develop in the near future) the force projection capability needed to invade any nation outside Asia. For this reason its espionage operations go largely unchecked by U.S. officials and policymakers. The PRC does, however, aggressively conduct espionage against the United States and a number of other industrialized nations.

The shortsighted allocation of America's intelligence resources has allowed the Chinese espionage apparatus to operate outside the focus of mainstream counterintelligence concerns. As a result the United States and other Western industrialized nations are woefully unprepared to protect their national assets from Beijing's espionage efforts. China's intelligence gathering operations have increased to the point where agencies with counterintelligence responsibilities are overwhelmed by the sheer number of cases. Not until recently has the U.S. intelligence community recognized the magnitude of China's efforts. Harry Godfrey III, chief of FBI counterintelligence, observed that

> "if we are talking about violations of U.S. law, the Chinese are surpassing the Russians. We know they are running operations here. We have seen cases where they have encouraged people to apply to the CIA, the FBI, Naval Investigative Service, and other Defense agencies. They have also attempted to recruit people at our [nuclear] research facilities at Los Alamos and at Lawrence Livermore."[3]

Like other regional or global powers, the leadership of the PRC bases its policies and actions on its military, political, and economic self-interests. Many of those interests involve reaping financial and technological benefits from close commercial ties with advanced industrialized nations. In recent years, China's human rights policies have alienated some of its former friends among the Western democracies and, in the case of the United States, restricted its access to some categories of advanced technology. China's intelligence services are therefore required to play a greater role in supporting national policy objectives by targeting and exploiting the technological, economic, political, and military infrastructures of the developed nations.

Industrial espionage and illegal technology transfers are only the most publicized aspects of China's intelligence activities. These types of operations are likely to receive greater emphasis in the future as China's foreign intelligence services continue to target the U.S. industrial sector. High-tech information; used to develop China's ailing civilian and military industrial sectors; is of particular importance to Beijing. As a result, the PRC's intelligence operations against the United States have become so intrusive that senior U.S. law enforcement officials have publicly identified China as "the most active foreign power engaged in the illegal acquisition of American technology."[4]

Espionage and other intelligence activities rarely require the proverbial cloak and dagger, but they are far more complicated than mere theft of a foreign government's classified materials. Espionage is an orchestrated, all-encompassing attempt to extract information from multiple levels of society. At the national level, desirable intelligence falls into several categories. Nations routinely collect and use volumes of data on foreign political situations, leadership figures, military force structures and capabilities, science and technology issues, economic conditions, and sociological factors. Each of these categories should be considered separately to piece together the true role of intelligence collection and analysis as practiced by the PRC:

Foreign political situations – All the affairs of state that determine a nation's future actions domestically and internationally.

Leadership figures – The histories and personalities of those individuals (military and civilian) who influence the affairs of state, now or in the future.

Military force structures and capabilities – Information such as the table of organization and equipment (TOE) for units of the armed forces; the locations, strengths, and missions of those units; and their ability to wage war.

Science and technology issues – The overall level of sophistication in civilian and military sectors as well as a society's ability to develop and use technology.

Economic conditions – Strengths and weaknesses of a nation's economy and how economic factors might influence domestic and foreign policies.

Sociological factors – Religious, cultural, and customary practices of a society and how those factors might affect its actions and decisions. (An example of this type of intelligence is the study of Vietnamese burial practices that was used to locate the remains of missing soldiers.)

In democratic societies much of this information is available in the open press. Indeed, the downfall of communism in eastern Europe and the former Soviet Union has unleashed a torrent of published information, most of it new to the West. In addition, a great deal of usable information can be gathered simply by watching a society function on a daily basis. General attitudes of the populace, political personalities and trends, and economic conditions are all topics addressed daily in any major Western newspaper. Intelligence agencies therefore spend considerable time and effort identifying, collecting, translating, and analyzing information from published open sources.

Information that cannot be found in open sources must be collected secretly via technical means: satellite imagery, communications intercepts, and the use of recruited agents. Clandestine intelligence operations are directed with equal vigilance against hard targets such as government political and military institutions and soft targets such as the industrial and academic sectors. The latter are referred to as "soft" because persons associated with these institutions usually lack knowledge of the operational methods of espionage and are therefore vulnerable to foreign penetration and exploitation.

My goal in this book is to identify China's national intelligence structure, objectives, and collection operations. I focus primarily on human-source intelligence (HUMINT) operations, which I analyze to determine China's intelligence strategies, methods, and capabilities. In addition, I also give some attention to the PRC's intelligence analysis community by identifying the roles and organization of major departments and agencies. For readers unfamiliar with intelligence terminology, a glossary of frequently used words and acronyms is provided.

Chapter 2

Framework
for Analysis

For the purposes of this study, human-source intelligence operations can be divided into three broad categories: overt, clandestine, and covert action. Overt intelligence activities are those collection and analysis functions that can be identified and attributed to a specific country. For example, when military attaches attend another country's military exercises they are engaged in overt intelligence collection. The host government expects that the attaches will report the event and any relevant information from it to their own governments. This information might include unit strengths, proficiency, procedures, equipment, tactics, and biographical data on commanders. In turn, the host government will attempt to gather information from the attending attaches – and they will do the same among themselves in the course of normal conversation. This type of activity, and other forms of direct observation and contact (e.g., a diplomat holding discussions with local inhabitants or government officials), is generally considered overt collection.

Clandestine activities are intelligence collection operations that, even if detected, cannot be attributed to a specific nation. These operations usually involve the recruitment of spies and are designed to hide the involvement of the nation that is behind them. For example, one might suspect clandestine collection activities if classified or restricted equipment was discovered in the hands of a third world nation that did not have the technical capability to produce it. One can assume that the equipment was stolen, although the thief and the exact method remain unknown.

Covert action operations are not intelligence collection activities per se. Instead, they are efforts such as economic and military assistance programs that are designed to manipulate a foreign government or other entity. Covert action operations can be divided into four general categories: political, economic, paramilitary, and those that feature disinformation.

All countries need various types of information to ensure their own security. And while there are substantial differences in national objectives, doctrines, and capabilities, the methods employed to collect and analyze information are virtually identical worldwide. This results in substantial similarities in the structures of intelligence services. This is not to say that every nation's intelligence units are organized along the same lines. However, the peculiar and generally clandestine nature of intelligence activities calls for certain operational and support services, and the departments that provide these essential services have a logical place in all organizations engaged in such activities.

Identifying the common administrative and functional bureaus within China's government agencies provides some insight into the structure of its civilian and military intelligence services. Governments generally create similar departments in each interlocking agency in order to achieve uniformity and to facilitate communication within the system. Like all government bureaucracies, the Chinese intelligence services must have a defined organizational structure to accomplish their various missions. In his study *Cadres, Bureaucracy, and Political Power in China,* noted sinologist A. Doak Barnett observed that China's government ministries have certain standard departments.[1] The hierarchical structure of authority in the PRC dictates that the roles and responsibilities of these common departments will be the same in each ministry.

Another source of information on the structure of China's intelligence apparatus is public exposure of clandestine operations. For the nonspecialist, analysis of publicly available information carries with it some dangers. Media accounts of a particular event can be tainted by a variety of outside influences, intentionally or inadvertently. First, a reporter's assessment of the meaning of the event may be inaccurate. For example, the publicly announced arrest of a spy by country X may mean very little to the reporter. But to the world's intelligence professionals it means that an espionage network set up by country Y has been compromised, along with the clandestine communication procedures, recruitment methods, and information objectives of country Y's intelligence service. It also means that country X's counterintelligence operation knew about the spy, probably for some time. This situation raises a number of important questions. How did country X know about the spy in its midst? When did it discover the spy? Was he or she fed false information to deceive country Y? If so, why was the counterintelligence operation ended and the arrest made public?

The public arrest of a spy brings into play the other possible influence on media reports: the influence wielded intentionally by a foreign government. Use of the press for the purpose of deception is particularly easy in a country like China, where the media is controlled. For this reason I exercised great care in looking at media reports. Almost all of the press accounts cited in this book were confirmed by persons with direct knowledge of the events in question.

Details of China's HUMINT collection operations – from press accounts and U.S. court and congressional records – highlight espionage techniques (or tradecraft), expose clandestine intelligence activities, and point to specific departments within China's intelligence agencies. By combining a schematic of the functional bureaus that provide intelligence-related services with an outline of the standard ministerial structure and then adding information from open sources, one can derive an accurate picture of the organization of the PRC's intelligence apparatus. With this done, the next task is to identify specific operations and methodologies by analyzing publicly available information about specific intelligence objectives and techniques.

To supplement the information obtained from open sources, dozens of interviews with Chinese dissidents, defectors, and active intelligence officers were conducted. Because of the security restrictions placed on me by the Department of Defense concerning contact with foreign nationals, I was initially unable to conduct several of these interviews. I therefore employed the services of an excellent researcher, Richard W. Marsh, Jr., who overcame many of the seemingly insurmountable problems inherent in interviewing persons who prefer not to be identified by their own government.

With the fear of persecution ever present, it became necessary to ensure anonymity to certain interviewees – particularly defectors from China's diplomatic corps, current intelligence officers, and recruited agents. To make these persons more difficult to identify I have used the third-person singular throughout. In the interest of academic integrity none of the material that they provided was taken at face value. Information about the activities and identities of Chinese intelligence officers was considered valid only if reported by at least two independent sources, or by a single source with a consistent reputation for reliability and firsthand knowledge of events.

Chapter 3

China's Information Objectives

In theory and general practice all intelligence activities, whether open or clandestine, are directed at either satisfying information requirements or covertly advancing national objectives. The former are known in intelligence circles as information objectives (IOs): specific requests for certain kinds of data, assigned to human or technical intelligence collectors by a nation's policy-making apparatus.

The information objectives of the PRC's leadership differ significantly from those of the global powers because of its unique strategic political and military concerns. In military terms the PRC is strictly a regional power, not a global power. General military policy in China has been under intense review since the early 1980s. Military officials there have shown considerable interest in the strategy and tactics used by the multinational coalition in the 1991 war against Iraq. However, the political leadership still relies primarily on the country's size and large population as a defense against perceived military threats from the outside world.

The PRC's perception of internal and external threats dictates the information requirements levied on its intelligence services. It has little to gain from intense espionage and analysis activities directed at global political-military alliances outside its region of influence. For military intelligence purposes, the PRC directs its resources toward identifying potential regional threats:

Commonwealth of Independent States – This new entity presents a significantly reduced military threat compared to its predecessor, the Soviet Union. However, historic animosity and territorial disputes still exist between China and the Russian republic. In addition, military and political instability in the new commonwealth concerns Beijing.

India – The long-standing distrust between this nation and the PRC is based on political differences, the 1962 border war, and the Chinese subjugation of Tibet.

Vietnam – Despite the recent rapprochement, tensions remain between Vietnam and the PRC because of Chinese hegemonic tendencies. China invaded Vietnam in 1979 to punish that country for its military occupation of Cambodia. Military and intelligence activities are still intense along the China-Vietnam border.

Muslim states north of Xinjian – The resurgence of fundamentalist Islam in the central Asian states of the former Soviet Union threatens to weaken Beijing's internal control over the Muslim population of Xinjian province. In 1990 the Chinese leadership used force to put down rebellious activity in the region.

Also of considerable interest to Beijing are American, Japanese, South Korean, and Taiwanese military activities along China's eastern seaboard and in the Sea of Japan.

China has less of an interest in the global political-military environment than nations with worldwide military commitments. Accordingly, the PRC continues to focus its intelligence collection activities on issues that more directly affect its internal stability, regional security, and technological and economic development.

In the fall of 1989 a new series of information objectives were handed to the PRC intelligence apparatus. The new IOs focus on specific strengths and weaknesses of the Bush administration's "campaign of peaceful evolution."[1]

The concerns that initiated the IOs were still prevalent in January 1992, when Chinese policymakers warned security services and Chinese Communist party (CPC) elements that "hostile forces and reactionary organizations overseas are carrying out mental offensives, sabotage activities, religious infiltration, fund [scholarship] infiltration, and cultural infiltration."[2]

This appears to be a direct reference to attempts by foreign governments to change China's behavior through increased contact and influence a policy advocated by the Bush and Clinton administrations.

The new IOs target the positions on Sino-American relations advocated by American institutions such as executive branch agencies (e.g., the State Department, the Commerce Department, the National Security Council) and members of Congress. It is logical to assume that collecting this information is a high priority, given China's interest in maintaining cordial relations with the United States. With this intelligence in hand, Chinese policymakers have recognized determined how to exploit differences between Congress and the executive, as this internal summary indicates:

> Bush's basic approach is to (1) maintain the status quo, (2) keep up the pressure, and (3) leave some latitude. The two sides share the same intention, and the difference lies in their assessment of the situation. We may make use of the difference between the two sides. Bush presses on the issue of overseas students and appeases on the issue of satellites.3

Overall, China's intelligence activities support its policy interests by acquiring foreign high technology (for military and civilian uses), identifying and influencing foreign policy trends (such as bilateral policy and trade issues), and monitoring dissident groups (such as democracy advocates and Taiwanese nationals).

Part Two
Ministry of
State Security

Chapter 4

Organizational Structure

China's preeminent civilian intelligence collection agency is the Guojia Anquan Bu, or Ministry of State Security (MSS). It was formed in June 1983 by combining the espionage, counterintelligence and security functions of the Ministry of Public Security (MPS), and the Investigations Department of the Chinese Communist party central committee.[1]

Prior to the reorganization China's leading intelligence service was the MPS, which still has a role in counterintelligence investigations and operations due to bureaucratic infighting and its pervasive presence at the lower levels of local government.[2]

The MSS is headed by the minister of state security, Jia Chunwang, who was appointed to fill the position in 1985.[3] Born in 1938, Jia is a native of Beijing and a 1964 graduate of the engineering physics department of Qinghua University. He is a member of the CPC central committee and had previously served as deputy secretary of the Beijing municipal committee and secretary of the Beijing Committee for Discipline Inspection.[4] He is reportedly a fan of the Central Intelligence Agency. The minister of state security, assisted by several deputy ministers, oversees all the bureaus within the ministry.

Each government ministry responsible for overseas operations has a foreign affairs bureau, and most such ministries also contain a separate Taiwan affairs department as well as a Hong Kong and Macao affairs office. China's premier foreign policy body, the Ministry of Foreign Affairs (MFA), is further subdivided into six geographic departments: African affairs, American and Oceanian affairs, Asian affairs, Soviet and East European affairs, West Asian and North African affairs, and West European affairs.[5]

Research institutes affiliated with the foreign affairs apparatus and intelligence agencies (including the MSS) use the same geographic divisions.[6] It would make sense, then, for the MSS to follow this pattern and have a foreign affairs bureau consisting of the standard geographic divisions, plus separate departments for Taiwan and Hong Kong/Macao.

Geographic divisions allow work units to specialize in a particular area of expertise but do not permit work to be accomplished by functional expertise. The structure of the MSS must therefore be divided not only by geographic considerations but by functional expertise as well. The next question then becomes what sorts of functional assets does the MSS need to conduct espionage and counterespionage in China and abroad?

First and foremost, it needs qualified personnel. Each employee must be recruited, screened, trained, paid, supplied, transported, fed, and occasionally housed. Support services such as logistics, records or database management, planning, and accounting are required as well. Most of the departments that provide these essential services can be found in all Chinese ministries.[7]

The universal practice within intelligence agencies of compartmentalizing information indicates that each of these services probably exists as a separate department in the MSS as well.

Doak Barnett's study emphasized that each minister is responsible for supervising all the work of that ministry, including that handled by its subordinate regional counterparts throughout the country.[8]

The standard bureaus and departments that perform routine administrative functions within virtually all PRC government ministries are as follows:

Personnel bureau – Staffed by CPC members, this office has tremendous influence in any ministry because of its role in personnel management and security issues.[9]

Policy study bureau – This unit is responsible for both short- and long-term planning for the ministry and the regional bodies under its supervision. It establishes work plans and expected levels of achievement.[10]

Finance and accounting – Frequently one of the larger administrative (as opposed to functional) bureaus, this work group is responsible for the general control and management of the ministry's finances.[11]

Training and education – This office is in charge of internal and external training for ministry personnel. Some ministries run schools for specialized instruction.[12]

The MSS's need to conceal its employees' identities and operational methodology dictates that the ministry has its own training program. The Beijing College of International Relations in 1965 closed during the cultural revolution and reopened in 1978, it is today the primary training facility for MSS personnel. Before it reopened, the Beijing College of International Politics (which was formally a part of the MPS) was the site for espionage training.[13]

Research institute – Ministries conducting any form of research maintain independent research institutes. The Institute of Contemporary International Relations is the analysis section of the MSS. In 1985 it had a staff of approximately three hundred researchers and support personnel. Work is divided according to the standard six geographic divisions (plus Taiwan and Hong Kong/Macao); there is also a division of global affairs. The institute publishes a classified journal, *Contemporary International Relations.*[14]

General affairs – Usually one of the larger departments within any ministry, this unit's wide range of responsibilities includes overseeing the supply section, the print shop, the library, the motor pool, and the housing and food management sections.[15]

Discipline inspection commission – The commission is the CPC central committee's representative body within any ministry. In the authoritative structure of the Chinese government, all ministries have party representation. The commission ensures loyalty by keeping the central committee informed on relevant matters. The People's Liberation Army (PLA) has a similar representative body – the General Political Department (GPD).

Secretariat – This office functions as the chief of staff and exists in all ministries. It serves as the central point for the assignment of tasks within the ministry and among other ministries. Acting on behalf of the ministry's director and deputy directors, it channels the flow of information and coordinates work priorities and schedules.[16]

With the administrative support structure in place, the ministry must also have a functional or operations department to conduct its mission (see fig. 2). Because the MSS is active domestically as well as abroad, operational sections and many support functions should be similarly divided. The result is that the MSS has separate departments at the bureau

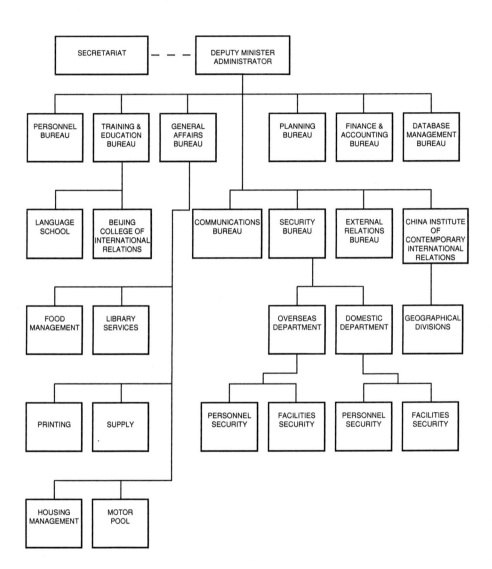

2. Ministry of State Security Administration

level for internal and external espionage investigations and operations. The fact that Yu Zhenshan identified as the former chief of the MSS's foreign affairs bureau, defected in 1986 confirmed the existence of such a structure.[17]

Public exposure of Chinese intelligence activities in Taiwan, Japan, and the United States – carried out by intelligence operatives posing as businessmen and diplomats – confirms that the MSS conducts clandestine collection operations overseas. It also indicates that the MSS is capable of fielding case officers under both official government (legal) covers and nongovernment (illegal) covers. In the case of the Chinese intelligence services, official cover has a wide range of applications. The PRC is represented overseas by accredited diplomats, trade and industry figures, commercial officers, military attaches, journalists, scientists, and students. Many of the aforementioned positions are used as legal cover for overseas espionage activities.

The use of legal covers by Chinese intelligence officers is a well-established practice in the global espionage trade. In a number of publicized spy scandals described later in this book, PRC intelligence officers (civilian and military) were exposed while operating under covers from the New China News Agency (NCNA), the Chinese People's Friendship Association, the Ministry of Foreign Affairs, the Ministry of National Defense, the United Front Works Department, the International Liaison Department, and official trade offices. The consistent use of legal covers over a long period (1960 to the present) is evidence of the depth of China's intelligence experience and its commitment to espionage as a tool of foreign policy.

China also makes extensive use of illegal covers. This is a more sophisticated and difficult method of operation because the case officer is not affiliated with his or her government. As a result a separate system of control and clandestine communication must be established to direct the illegal operative and receive information in return. This process is dangerous for the illegal case officer because he or she has no diplomatic immunity. If this individual is caught by a foreign government, he or she usually faces imprisonment – or worse. Recent espionage cases in the United States and Taiwan provide firsthand examples of how China uses illegal networks.

In February 1986 retired CIA employee Larry Wu-tai Chin was convicted of espionage. Some question exists as to whether Chin was a bona fide illegal case officer or simply a recruited agent. But according to court records, Chin was awarded the rank of deputy bureau chief in the Ministry of Public Security.[18]

He worked in the U.S. intelligence community for approximately thirty-five years. All the while, he was providing classified information to the PRC.

In June 1988 Liu Kuangsheng was arrested in Taipei and charged with sedition and espionage on behalf of the mainland Chinese government. Subsequent investigations revealed that in 1986 Liu had failed in an attempt to enter Taiwan using a false Thai passport. One year later, he successfully entered the country using a false Singaporean passport and established an overseas trading company. According to Taiwanese authorities, Liu was a professional intelligence officer sent to build a long-term espionage network on Taiwan.[19]

A similar case was that of Tung Li, who in 1987 was convicted of espionage on behalf of the PRC in Taipei. Li had entered Taiwan in 1986 on a false Singaporean passport. He had established a trading company and was engaging in what Taiwanese officials described as "united front" economic tactics, a reference to the Chinese Communist doctrine of joining forces with another entity against a mutually perceived threat. He was uncovered by security authorities after he filled out a business application form inadvertently using simplified Chinese characters – the writing system used on the mainland.[20]

Like Liu Kuangsheng, Tung Li was a professional intelligence officer.

A close examination of the Liu Kangsheng and Tung Li cases provides more insight into the structure and capabilities of the MSS. Liu used false Thai and Singaporean passports, and Li also carried a forged Singaporean passport. In both cases the passports were reportedly falsified documents, not altered originals.[21]

The reproduction of passports is an expensive process – and in the case of the Thai example, a difficult one as well. (Thai passports have multiple security features such as a photolaminate layer, a wet seal, a dry seal, and a signature strip.) So it is logical to assume that the MSS has significant photographic, artistic, and printing capabilities if it can provide false documents of this quality to its intelligence operatives. Additional technical support sent to its field operatives includes chemicals for invisible messages, covert communication devices, encryption and decryption codes, and photographic equipment.

The PRC's detailed knowledge of these types of espionage techniques comes out in its public announcements of counterespionage successes. In press reports MSS representatives have claimed that spies from Taiwan and other foreign powers have been caught in possession

of the aforementioned equipment by various provincial MSS offices.[22]
Such reports lead to five conclusions:

1. The MSS has the operational knowledge to provide technical support for espionage operations.
2. The MSS has a public or external affairs unit.
3. The national MSS supervises the provincial offices.
4. In domestic counterespionage, the MSS has an investigative role.
5. MSS officers are trained to identify the operational tactics and technical equipment used to conduct espionage.

The MSS's current structure can be seen in greater clarity when juxtaposed with the known activities of the MPS. The MPS's political security section used to conduct counterespionage operations against foreign intelligence services. It was also responsible for counterintelligence investigations of citizens who had traveled overseas or maintained foreign contacts.[23]

The difference between counterintelligence investigations and counter-espionage operations is noteworthy. The former entails interviewing people and collecting documentary and physical evidence. It is a discreet but relatively open activity designed to identify recruited agents and foreign espionage activities. Counterespionage operations involve the recruitment of agents and are designed to penetrate foreign intelligence organizations in order to collect information and manipulate the adversary.

Since it inherited its counterespionage role from the MPS, it is likely that the MSS organizes its domestic operations along the same lines. A diagram of its known overseas and domestic activities reveals more of the MSS's intelligence structure (see fig. 3).

A sampling of the world press further indicates the wide reach of China's overseas clandestine espionage operations. Such operations have been uncovered – and publicly exposed – in the Sudan in 1964, Malawi in 1965, Kenya in 1965, the Central African Republic in 1966, Brazil in 1964 and 1977, France in 1983, and the United States in 1985 and 1987.[24]

In each case, the intelligence officer operated under the cover of a New China News Agency journalist, official trade office representative, military attaché, or accredited diplomat. Because conducting clandestine operations in foreign countries requires certain support services unique to the intelligence industry, it follows that China's espionage

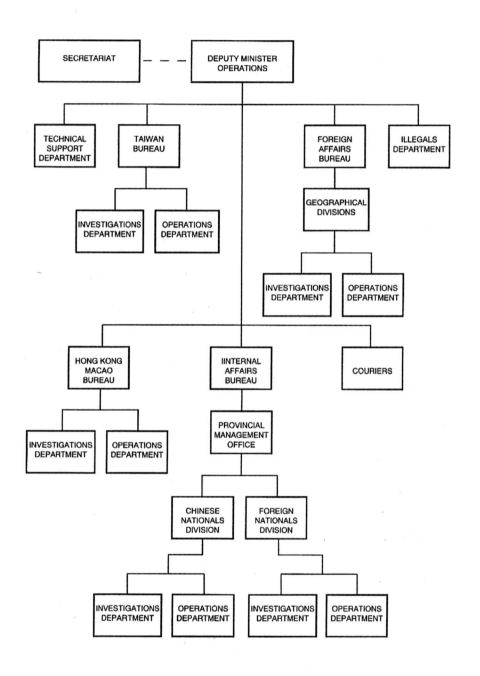

figure 3, Ministry of State Security Operations

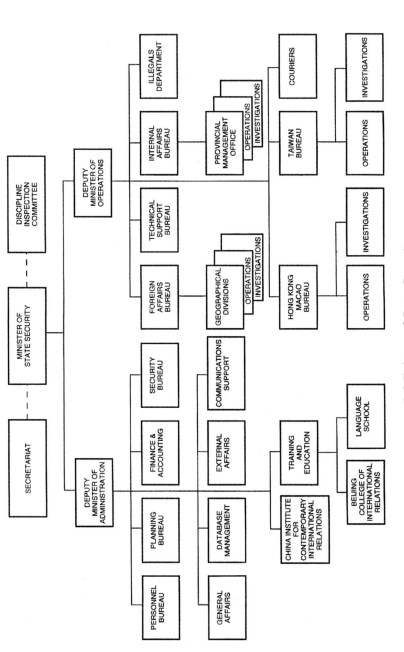

4. Ministry of State Security

apparatus performs these support services as well.

The MSS operates in foreign countries under a variety of covers. Because the role of case officers is to recruit, train, and handle informants, they must be able to speak and read a variety of languages. They must also be capable of translating foreign documents. The Chinese foreign affairs apparatus puts tremendous emphasis on the language abilities of its officers.[25]

So it is likely that the MSS maintains some type of language training program under its training and education office. Translation services probably exist in a separate department closely tied to the China Institute of Contemporary International Relations. Once an MSS case officer obtains information from an agent, that information must be sent to Beijing. This can be done via the secure transmission facilities available at the embassy, in which case a communications officer would be needed. An alternative method of relaying information – the one used by Larry Chin – is to employ a courier.[26]

This would be the preferred method when the data is not time sensitive and when contact with an embassy official or another representative of a foreign country (such as news agency or trade office personnel) might attract unwanted interest from the host government's counterintelligence service. In any case, both communication methods involve specialized support functions.

Another characteristic of intelligence organizations is the existence of a powerful security department. In most Chinese government ministries, responsibility for security is relegated to the general affairs department.[27]

These operations consist of physical safeguards, access control (requiring ID badges, for example), and technical and information security programs. The exaggerated need for security in the MSS makes it likely that the security function exists as a separate department. Intelligence services aggressively target employees of their counterparts in other nations for recruitment purposes. Therefore, security operations and procedures play very important roles in any intelligence unit. Certain procedures must be followed when handling information, building new facilities, and associating with foreign nationals. Another reason for the MSS to maintain a large security department is that it inherited some of the MPS's security responsibilities.[28]

It must also have some control over the security of its personnel and facilities both in China and overseas. Logically, those functions would be assigned to separate units within the agency.

The organizational structure of the MSS indicates that the agency runs a wide range of administrative and functional operations both domestically and overseas (see fig. 4). One can only speculate about the existence of other mission-oriented bureaus within the MSS. It is particularly difficult to identify the exact titles – as opposed to the functions – of bureaus and departments because their designations are changed periodically to enhance security.[29]

Analysis of the structure, however, produces only an assessment of the organization's roles and capabilities. To identify its operational methodology, one must study published accounts of clandestine intelligence activities. The espionage tradecraft can next be analyzed and compared to the organization's structure to determine its information objectives and HUMINT capabilities.

Chapter 5

Foreign Operations

The operational methodology of the Chinese intelligence services is nothing new to espionage. It is, however, uniquely Chinese in its application. To collect information, the MSS co-opts vast numbers of Chinese citizens living or traveling overseas. Senior U.S. counter-intelligence officials compare the method to classical Soviet espionage techniques, which used fewer people but gathered more information. The Chinese approach poses many problems for U.S. law enforcement efforts, according to FBI counterintelligence chief Harry Godfrey III: "For prosecutive purposes, you are looking at an individual collecting one small part one time, and you don't have the quality of case that our country will take to prosecute as far as espionage."[1]

Most Chinese clandestine collection activities are not sophisticated operations, but their numbers compensate for this weakness. To conduct espionage in the United States the MSS draws on the services of the following:

— 1,500 Chinese diplomats and commercial representatives
— 70 PRC establishments and offices
— 15,000 Chinese students arriving annually
— 10,000 representatives traveling in 2,700 delegations each year
— a large ethnic Chinese community[2]

In recent years the PRC's clandestine collection operations in the United States have expanded to the point where approximately 50 percent of the nine hundred technology transfer cases investigated annually on the West Coast involve the Chinese.[3] This figure is interesting when examined in the context of the list compiled by the Justice Department's Export Control Enforcement Unit, Internal Security Section, and published as Significant Export Control Cases from January 1981 to May 1992.

Statistical analysis of the Department of Justice list indicates that only 6 percent of 272 significant cases involved China, and that 62.5 percent of those cases occurred on the West Coast. In addition, 13.4 percent of the incidents listed in *Department of Commerce Export Enforcement Cases: Closed January 1, 1986, to March 31, 1993*, involved the PRC. Much of China's espionage efforts in industrialized nations and focused on midlevel technology not cleared for export. Illegal acquisition of such items draws less interest from U.S. law enforcement agencies and judicial organs (i.e., state and federal prosecutors and the courts) than does the theft of state-of-the-art technology. For that reason the PRC's technology-related intelligence collection operations have gone relatively unimpeded.

Computer-assisted analysis of China's exposed technology-related espionage activities in the United States reveals three basic operational patterns. First, co-optees are recruited in China and asked to acquire the targeted technologies while they travel abroad. Second, American companies with access to the desired level of technology are purchased outright by Chinese state-run firms. In intelligence circles this is considered a bold or aggressive operation. Third and most commonly, high-technology equipment is purchased by recruited agents running front companies in Hong Kong.

China's most productive method of legally acquiring foreign technology is to send scientists overseas on scholarly exchange programs.[4]

Each year several thousand Chinese citizens travel to the United States for trade missions, scientific cooperation programs, and the like. It is a normal, "open" intelligence procedure to debrief the returning delegates to determine whether useful information was acquired by simple observation. However, the MSS and military intelligence services further exploit these opportunities by co-opting a number of these travelers to carry out specific operational activities. Frequently these activities involve passing messages or collecting information.

This method of clandestine collection became public in the United States on 29 September 1988, the day the PRC detonated its first neutron bomb. According to the subsequent FBI investigation, the technology required to produce the device did not originate in China but instead was acquired from Lawrence Livermore National Laboratory in Livermore, California.[5]

During the mid-1980s security at the facility was lax, and various delegations – composed ostensibly of Chinese scientists – had visited the facility without appropriate background checks. The FBI's investigation determined that several of the visiting scientists either had strong ties to the MSS or were in fact intelligence officers.[6] The MSS could easily have recruited an agent at Lawrence Livermore during one of these visits.

The process of obtaining information via scientific or trade delegations is a common form of low-level espionage. But as the Lawrence Livermore case indicates, it can also be quite effective in gathering otherwise unattainable data. In addition, the presence of PRC intelligence officers on scholarly or scientific exchange programs serves other purposes: (1) to identify and collect biographical data on personnel with access to needed information who could be subject to recruitment, (2) to gather information on government or industrial facilities and programs, and (3) to monitor the activities of the Chinese nationals in attendance for security and counterintelligence concerns.

The operational differences between professional intelligence officers and co-opted individuals are often noticeable. The intelligence officer generally has less technical knowledge about the subject matter involved in the operation, while the co-optee usually has no expertise in collecting information clandestinely. For example, at a trade show in Paris military investigators observed members of a Chinese scientific delegation discreetly dipping their ties in a photo processing solution made by the German firm Agfa.[7]

The goal of this clumsy act of espionage was presumably to obtain specimens of the solution for later analysis. Technology-related clandestine intelligence activities are by no means limited to scientific and trade delegations. The PRC has attempted to purchase U.S. firms with access to high technology not authorized for release to foreign countries. In February 1990 the United States, citing national security concerns, ordered the China National Aero-Technology Import & Export Corp. (CATIC) to divest itself of Mamco Manufacturing Inc., a Seattle aircraft parts manufacturer.[8]

The Bush administration said publicly that CATIC had a "checkered history" and had sought technology that would provide the Chinese People's Liberation Army's Air Force with in-flight refueling capabilities. More disturbing to administration officials was the belief that CATIC used Mamco as a front to penetrate other, more promising areas of restricted technology.[9]

The purchase of Mamco cannot be linked definitively to MSS

operations based on the information made public. However, intelligence services determine their information collection priorities in response to specific requests made by government and military consumers. To avoid costly duplication of effort, they must remain aware of ongoing collection activities. For that reason it is inconceivable that a large-scale activity with such significant intelligence potential as the purchase of a foreign company with access to high technology could occur without the knowledge and approval of the MSS. Its involvement would be required to research the history of the company and to evaluate its potential as a vehicle for gaining access to otherwise unattainable information.

Such large-scale intelligence activities necessarily involve other defense agencies because of the level of scientific and technical knowledge required. For example, the attempted purchase of Mamco by CATIC would almost certainly have involved the Commission of Science, Technology, and Industry for National Defense (COSTIND). The commission's primary responsibilities are the supervision of weapons research and development and the coordination of the military-industrial complex with civilian sectors of society.[10]

The purchase of a large American company is a rare operation compared to the more frequent intelligence activities of the MSS, which generally procures restricted technology through more subtle and clandestine means. It appears that the most effective means of stealing foreign technology involves the use of recruited agents in Hong Kong. Examination of several public cases of attempted (and successful) thefts of high technology reveals a unique pattern of operation. The recruited agent establishes a front company in Hong Kong. The company may in fact carry on legitimate trading activities in addition to illegally purchasing and shipping technology. The agent approaches several U.S. firms and tries to purchase restricted high-tech equipment – either in person at trade shows, over the phone, or by fax (the latter two methods offer the agent more security). Subsources within the target country can be used to facilitate purchasing and shipping transactions.

This operational method was employed in February 1984 by Hong Kong businessman Da Chuan Zheng. While attempting to illegally acquire and transport advanced radar and electronic surveillance technology to the PRC, Zheng and his accomplices, Kuang Shin Lin, David Tsai, Kwong Allen Yeung, and Jing-Li Zhang, were arrested by U.S. customs agents. Lin had boasted to undercover officers that he had shipped more than $25 million worth of high-tech equipment to the PRC. Andrew K. Ruotolo, Jr., the federal prosecutor in charge of the case, revealed that Zheng and his associates had made other contacts in Massachusetts, Virginia, and California in attempts to secure similar strategic materials.[11]

The Zheng case is not unusual. In recent years a number of similar cases have been reported in the press. From January 1983 to March 1984 Bernardus J. Smit of the Berkeley-based Dual Systems Control Corp. shipped seventy microcomputers from the United States to China, via Hong Kong, in violation of the Export Control Act. In another case, an illegal shipment of computers was sent from the United States to the PRC by Hong Kong middleman Hon Kwan Yu, doing business as Seed H.K. Ltd. Both front companies used the same address: 7/F Cheung Kong Building, 661 Kings Road, North Point, Hong Kong.[12]

The persistent use of Hong Kong as a transfer point is significant because it reveals a pattern of operation. As of March 1992 the U.S. Department of Commerce had thirty-three Hong Kong-based companies on its list of firms denied export privileges for illegally transferring high technology to the PRC.[13]

Examination of the department's denial orders identifies several instances where two or more Hong Kong-based firms share a single address. This is one indication that the companies may exist in name only and may serve as covers for espionage activities.

A unique characteristic of MSS technology transfer operations is that the recruited agent is often relatively honest with his American counterpart as to the final destination of the product. This may be attributed to poor espionage tradecraft, or perhaps to the Hong Kong Chinese mentality that all is fair in business. In fact, after reviewing these cases one is left with the distinct impression that Chinese businessmen see the illegal transfer of high technology not as a criminal act but as a simple business transaction. Lenient fines and prison sentences handed down by U.S. courts tend to support that attitude.

For those occasions when the operation is conducted in a truly clandestine manner, the Commerce Department lists several indicators of illegal technology diversion schemes, some of which are applicable to MSS methodology:

1. The customer or purchasing agent is reluctant to discuss the end use of a product.

2. The buyer offers to pay cash for a very expensive item when the terms of the sale call for financing.
3. The customer declines routine installation, training, or maintenance services.
4. A freight forwarding firm is listed as the product's final destination.
5. questioned, the buyer is evasive – especially about whether the purchased product is for reexport.[14]

While acquiring advanced technology is a high priority for the PRC, it is not the only focus of clandestine collection activities by the MSS overseas. The ministry has demonstrated a strong interest in penetrating U.S. government agencies and Chinese dissident organizations. Perhaps the most publicized – and most damaging – case of Chinese espionage against the United States is that of former CIA analyst Larry Wu-tai Chin (Jin Wudai).

From 1944 to 1981 Chin worked for the U.S. government. For thirty of those years he was a Chinese linguist and analyst for the CIA. In November 1985 Chin was indicted on six espionage-related charges and eleven counts of income tax fraud and evasion.[15]

Chin was recruited by the Chinese intelligence apparatus in 1944 while he was working for the U.S. Army liaison office in Fuzhou, China.[16]

From 1945 to 1952 he was a translator for the American consulates in Shanghai and Hong Kong and an interpreter for the Army in Korea, where he helped to debrief POWs. After 1952 he went to the CIA's Foreign Broadcast Information Service (FBIS) in Okinawa (1952-61); Santa Rosa, California (1961-71); and Rosslyn, Virginia (1971-81).[17]

In the course of his nearly forty-year espionage career, Chin supplied the PRC with information on U.S. intelligence requirements and foreign policy initiatives relating to China, as well as a biographical profile of at least one CIA co-worker, Victoria Loo.[18]

In one specific instance he confessed to having passed a classified document to Beijing in October 1970 that discussed President Nixon's desire to open relations with the PRC.[19]

China's leadership therefore knew about Nixon's intentions well in advance of his diplomatic overtures. This would have allowed the country to alter its internal and external policies (such as the volume of anti-U.S. rhetoric in the press) in order to reap the maximum political benefits.

As an FBIS analyst and one of the CIA's few fluent Chinese linguists, Chin was able to pass along such information as Intelligence Information Reports (IIRs) on China and East Asia, biographical profiles and assessments of fellow CIA employees, and the names and identities of the agency's covert employees. He was also in a position to provide information about recruited agents in China. Due to the CIA's internal policy of compartmentalization, Chin did not know their real names or identities; however, based on the intelligence they provided he could infer such things as their locations, employers, and levels of access. Chinese counterespionage and security operations could then attempt to identify them by determining who had access to the information that was being forwarded to the Americans. Once the agents were identified, they would routinely be arrested or fed false information to be communicated to the CIA.

Certain reasonable assumptions regarding U.S. intelligence activities can be made on the basis of Chin's actions and the types of information known to have been passed to the PRC:

1. The MSS could have determined how accurate U.S. intelligence assessments concerning China's intelligence, political, economic, and military infrastructures were.
2. Beijing has a strong interest in obtaining information about U.S. secure communications. This is indicated by the favorable response that Chin received when he claimed to the MSS that he had a contract job at the National Security Agency and provided a synopsis of James Bamford's book *The Puzzle Palace*.
3. A number of U.S. intelligence and counterintelligence activities were compromised.
4. A number of CIA employees are targeted for recruitment by China's intelligence services.
5. Before 1981 American and allied intelligence efforts were not successful at penetrating either the MPS or the MSS at a level high enough to detect Chin's clandestine activities.

Effective penetration of China's espionage apparatus has proven elusive for many foreign intelligence services, including those of the former Soviet Union. On numerous occasions from the 1970s to the mid-1980s the Soviet Committee for State Security (KGB) berated its overseas field stations (*residentzia*) for recruiting very few agents inside China's intelligence and policy agencies.[20]

This shortcoming was attributed to effective Chinese counterintelligence and security practices:

> As a result of the extremely harsh police regime in the PRC, and the total surveillance by the special services of Chinese officials, including those in establishments abroad, the Chinese as a whole lead an ascetic form of life to avoid reprisals, and do not deviate from the prescribed rules of behavior in the presence of compatriots.[21]

The KGB's assessment of the behavior of Chinese officials is still valid. The primary security rule imposed by the MSS on all government employees serving overseas is to travel in pairs. Before embarking on an overseas assignment, all personnel are informed of their responsibility to identify any employee who does not adhere to security regulations.[22]

This policy is designed to ensure around-the-clock surveillance of government workers and to minimize opportunities for foreign intelligence recruitment. Based on our knowledge of the PRC's security regulations and our analysis of the Chin case, we can infer that operations security (OPSEC) is practiced effectively by China's intelligence and policy agencies. Simply put, OPSEC is the application of security procedures to any activity. The procedures are designed to deny the enemy knowledge of, or critical information about, ongoing operations. Regarding the Chin case, in almost forty years China never took actions or instituted policies that betrayed its policymakers' advance knowledge of U.S. intentions (which in this case would include U.S.-conducted intelligence operations as well as military, economic, and diplomatic policies).

Public sources have attributed the exposure of Chin's espionage activities to the 1985 defection of Yu Zhensan, chief of the MSS's foreign affairs bureau. Because Chin was retired, a standard security clearance update would not have brought his earlier activities to light. In addition, during a November 1985 interview Chin remarked to FBI special agent Mark R. Johnson that the detailed information the FBI possessed could only have come from a high-level source within the Chinese government. But trial transcripts indicate that FBI and Treasury Department probes were already under way in early 1982. In fact, the U.S. Customs

Service recorded Chin's room-key number while searching his luggage when he returned from a February 1982 trip to Beijing.[23]

This meticulous procedure is known as a "full Customs search" and is not done unless someone is identified as a suspect in a criminal investigation in the Customs Service's airport computer, the Treasury Enforcement Communication System (TECS).[24] The FBI must have identified Chin to Customs sometime in 1981. So either Yu Zhensan was recruited by the United States as a controlled agent before 1982, or the United States or an allied government had another high-level agent with the proper access in the PRC intelligence apparatus. For security reasons, only a few high-level intelligence personnel would have had knowledge of Chin's actual identity. It is therefore likely that Yu was a recruited U.S. agent by 1981.

Analysis of the Chin case reveals much about the PRC's information requirements concerning the United States. Based on his criteria for selecting documents and on the data he is known or suspected to have turned over to Beijing, the general objectives are as follows:

1. Information about diplomatic, political, and economic policies toward the PRC
2. knowledge of foreign intelligence operations directed at China
3. Information about U.S. information requirements concerning the PRC
4. Biographical profiles of U.S. intelligence officers
5. Details of secure communications capabilities[25]

Further analysis of the Chin case identifies the MSS's standard espionage techniques. For example, Chin dropped off classified data while in Canada and in Hong Kong. The method, whereby an agent or illegal operative passes information and receives instructions through another country, is known as a third-country controlled operation or an external espionage net. The net operates within the target country, but the case officer who runs it lives and operates in a third country. This gives the case officer a high degree of security.[26]

The agent generally travels to the third country only for brief periods, which prevents the target government's counterintelligence service from detecting the espionage activity. Chin met his contact – Mr. Lee – in a Toronto shopping mall for approximately five minutes each time.[27]

Under the third-country control method the only overt sign of intelligence activity is the operative's overseas travels, which are often explained as vacations. Chin's primary operational activities – passing classified data and receiving instructions—usually took place in countries other than mainland China. On at least six occasions he passed undeveloped film to his MSS courier in the same Toronto mall. At other times he was debriefed by Chinese case officers in Hong Kong.[28] The MSS's preference for debriefing individuals as opposed to nonpersonal forms of clandestine communication is demonstrated by its handling of other agents as well (see Chapter 7).[29]

When he had something to deliver, Chin would first send a letter to an accommodation address in one of three locations: Canton, Guangdong, or Hong Kong. The letter cryptically stated when and where he would arrive in a third country.[30] This form of espionage tradecraft does not allow for speedy transmittal of data but is more secure than similar attempts inside the target country. However, as the case of the Nixon policy document illustrates, Chin also had a way to relay information quickly in the event of an emergency.[31] In addition, the use of third-country control techniques suggests that Chinese intelligence services are aware of U.S. counterintelligence capabilities.

The use of third-country control operations is a fundamental element of Chinese espionage methodology. From the 1950s to the present successive Chinese intelligence services have directed clandestine and open collection activities as well as covert operations against the United States from bases in England and other European nations. As part of these covert action programs, Americans and Europeans collaborated with Chinese security agencies to influence U.S. public opinion. For nearly three decades, propagandistic material from the Beijing Foreign Language Press and the International Bookstore was shipped from P.O. Box 88 in Beijing to the United States and England via recruited agents in various cities in Europe.

These programs were particularly active during the Vietnam War, when – in addition to implementing a large-scale propaganda campaign – Americans working as Chinese agents organized numerous antiwar campus sit-ins and demonstrations in the United States.[32] At the request of the Central Committee of the Communist party, Chinese intelligence recruited a number of American academics and students to work on eliminating U.S. involvement in Southeast Asia.[33]

Many leaders of the group discussed strategy at frequent meetings in Beijing:

There were suggestions about making recordings to send to
North Vietnam and South Vietnam. In South Vietnam they
would be broadcast to American soldiers. Others suggested writing letters and propaganda sheets and getting those to America by various means. A select committee was appointed to provide the means. They wanted to bring as many professors and
students as possible into the chain. The Chinese envisioned that
the start would be made on the campuses; the Party saw the
war coming to a halt because of this movement in America.[34]

In addition to formulating covert action operations, Chinese intelligence services actively collect open-source information from the
United States from individuals (or cutouts) and mailing addresses in
Europe. Prior to China's establishment of diplomatic relations with the
United States and its opening to the West, Chinese intelligence used
recruited agents living in Europe to gather data from American busi-
nesses, industries, universities, publishing houses, and technical societies.[35]

Often the information was not classified; but as was discussed
above, open-source publications and commercial, scientific, and technical data are valuable forms of intelligence.

Compared to the Vietnam-era covert operations and the open-source
collection efforts, the Chin case reveals dramatically different intelligence
objectives. For one thing, it clearly illustrates the MSS's desire to penetrate the U.S. intelligence apparatus. Other recent publicly exposed
espionage cases tend to support this thesis as well. In December 1987
two Chinese diplomats were expelled from the United States for activities incompatible with their diplomatic status. The two men – Hou
Desheng, an assistant military attaché based in Washington, D.C., and
Zhang Weichu, the Chinese consul in Chicago – were arrested in a
Washington restaurant attempting to purchase what they believed to be
classified National Security Agency documents.[36]

The NSA is America's premier agency for intercepting foreign communications and protecting U.S. diplomatic and military transmis-
sions. The two Chinese case officers unknowingly made contact not
with an NSA employee, but with an FBI double agent.

Another attempt by the PRC to penetrate the American intelligence community occurred in November 1988. A State Department
communications officer was removed from his assignment at the American embassy in Beijing after a recruitment attempt by the MSS.[37] This

attempt was significant because if it had succeeded the PRC would have had access to all embassy communications.

Taken as a whole, these recruitment attempts and Larry Chin's actions clearly show that the Chinese intelligence apparatus is working aggressively to penetrate U.S. secure communication systems. These represent the most sensitive (and as a result the most well protected) area of diplomatic, intelligence, and military operations. A single well-placed agent in a foreign communications agency might provide the information necessary to decipher millions of messages.

These cases also point to tendencies in Chinese espionage tradecraft. American law enforcement and intelligence officials have generally promoted the notions that PRC collection operations primarily employ Americans of Chinese descent and that the focus of such operations is high technology. The previous cases demonstrate conclusively that neither proposition is entirely true. The MSS actively targets and seeks to penetrate American intelligence and policy-making agencies. Moreover, given the numbers of recently exposed intelligence operations directed at the United States, it is logical to conclude that the PRC has had at least some success in recruiting and maintaining controlled agents in these agencies.

Another high-priority objective for the MSS is monitoring Chinese dissident groups, many of which formed in response to the Tiananmen Square incident in June 1989. Overseas Chinese students and dissidents in Japan, Europe, and the United States have reported being harassed, threatened, and watched by PRC embassy and consular officials.[38]

There is substantive evidence that the Chinese government has initiated a campaign of surveillance and harassment on two levels, covert and overt. For its part, the MSS actively infiltrates prodemocracy dissident groups. Senior members of the Washington, D.C.-based International Federation of Chinese Scholars and Students (IFCSS) stated that numerous MSS agents identified themselves to dissident leaders immediately after the Tiananmen incident.[39]

The MSS's technique of covertly infiltrating student and dissident organizations became public in June 1989, when a delegate to the Chinese Alliance for Democracy convention in California publicly declared that he was a spy and severed his ties to the MSS. Shau Huaqiang was recruited by provincial MSS officers before he came to the United States. He was required to sign an agreement to spy on behalf of the MSS as the price for being permitted to make the trip. He was ordered to infiltrate the alliance, disrupt its work, and uncover evidence of a financial link with Taiwan.[40]

Prodemocracy advocates believe there are still MSS agents within their organizations, and a number of disruptive incidents tend to support that belief. For example, while en route to a prodemocracy demonstration in Washington, D.C., buses from Boston and New York had their tires slashed. Membership lists are sometimes stolen, and dissidents have received threatening letters (often an AK-47 bullet is enclosed in the envelope) and phone calls.[41]

As the case of Shau Huaqiang demonstrates, these types of covert acts of sabotage fit the general intelligence objectives tasked to low-level MSS agents recruited to work against dissident movements.

On a more open level, pressure is applied to Chinese dissidents primarily through their family members in the PRC. Student dissident leaders have testified before Congress about how the Chinese government monitors their mail and about the threats to family members made by provincial MPS officials. The gist of these stories is generally the same. Incoming letters from overseas Chinese students are opened or confiscated by public security officials. If the letters contain any information deemed threatening to the state, family members are called in to explain the contents. They are threatened with the loss of their jobs and instructed to tell the student to cease involvement in dissident activities.[42]

The fact that families are approached by MPS officers and not MSS personnel indicates that the two agencies have definite jurisdictional boundaries and that they coordinate their efforts. As an element of the Communist party, the Political Legal Leading Committee (PLLC) is responsible for coordinating dissident suppression and all other counterespionage activities in China. The MPS maintains some responsibility for counterespionage investigations thanks to bureaucratic infighting and to the fact that it is represented at the lowest levels of government. Information collected by the MSS on Chinese dissidents overseas goes from the national PLLC to subordinate offices at the provincial level. The provincial offices send their cases to either the MPS or the MSS, depending on the course of action recommended by the party and the availability of resources.[43]

Along with the threats to family members, open harassment of dissidents includes the nonrenewal of visas and passports and the termination of educational grants – steps that are arguably reasonable for a government to take if it feels threatened by overseas dissidents. The harassment campaigns uncovered in the United States were conducted by PRC embassy education department employees as part of what appears to be a poorly executed attempt to control dissident activities. Embassy officials would interview Chinese students about the prodemocracy movement. When student leaders were identified, they were denied financial assistance, visa renewals, future employment, and access to embassy support services such as transportation and financial aid; in some cases they were threatened as well.[44]

Similar patterns of behavior by Chinese embassy employees have been reported in Japan, Australia, and throughout Europe. In May 1990, Xu Lin, a third secretary in the education section of the embassy in Washington, D.C., defected to the United States, citing fear of imprisonment to justify his request for asylum.[45] Xu had refused to participate in the what he described as the PRC's harassment campaign and would not provide embassy-based MSS officers with unsigned informant letters identifying prodemocracy dissidents and their activities. Presumably the anonymous letters are an unsophisticated method of secret communication between agents and case officers. In his testimony before Congress, Xu described the education department's role in monitoring and hounding democracy activists as separate from the ongoing activities of the MSS:

The department frequently engaged itself in threat and intimidation on the students who continued to be involved in the pro-democracy movement and set up a variety of archives to keep track of student leaders, pro-democracy activists and the students who openly renounced their Communist party membership. The information collected was promptly sent back to China through diplomatic messengers or secret codes. The department also intervened in the activities and elections of associations of Chinese students and scholars and tried to restore or set up branches of the Communist party. While using what is known as professional students sent by the government to monitor student activities, it also tried to recruit pro-government students to collect information.[46]

Xu disclosed that as an embassy official one of his primary tasks was to pressure Chinese students not to support a revocation of most-favored-nation (MFN) trading status for China. He reported that it was the "habitual practice" of embassy officials to pressure students not to publish prodemocracy statements or articles, or to participate in demonstrations. The methods of intimidation usually involved threats (1) of the loss of one's job and the possibility of any future in China, and (2) of reprisals against family members still in the PRC.[47]

When he defected, Xu brought documentary evidence that Beijing instructed its embassies' education departments systematically to intimidate student dissidents and to disrupt their activities. According to one of the documents Xu provided (see appendix 1), China's state education commission convened a meeting of educational counselors in March 1990. Officials of the MPS and MSS briefed the educators on the Front for Democratic China, the Chinese Alliance for Democracy, and other prodemocracy groups. As a result of this policy-making conference, embassies in the United States and Canada were ordered to initiate efforts to control dissident Chinese scholars and students:

The first thing on our agenda is to control Party organizations; the second is to control the Friendship Association of Chinese Students and Scholars. Our demands should not be too high or pressing. We can work like underground organizations, find a few reliable ones in each school and form a Party branch. The backbone members can stay abroad.[48]

Xu Lin said that overseas "the intelligence service, which operates from the embassy, also aggressively targets Chinese students."[49]

The clandestine collection and covert action roles of the MSS are separate from those intelligence activities conducted by the educational affairs department.[50] Diplomatic personnel in the education departments, therefore, act as co-opted assets by conducting intelligence operations against Chinese student dissidents overseas.

The PRC policy documents provided by Xu Lin contain a great deal of information about prodemocracy activists. The detailed analysis and guidance sent from Chinese policymakers to embassy personnel suggest that the MSS has been effective in penetrating and collecting information about overseas dissident groups. For example, the documents divide prodemocracy activists into five categories. Each category is based on the individual's feelings toward the PRC government as reflected by his or her level of involvement in prodemocracy activities. The categories are as follows:

A. First category: People in this category have a higher political awareness and a more correct understanding of antigovernment activities. . . . Some of them may, according to our needs, continue to stay abroad to study or work in order to give full play to their political role and their role of uniting and organizing overseas students and scholars. . . .

B. Second category: People in this category have some patriotism, and they hope their socialist motherland will prosper and become strong. But in the near future these people will not fully agree with our government's principles and policies. But they do not oppose our government from the fundamental political perspective. . . .

C. Third category: People in this category are ideologically more deeply influenced by Western values and hold politically different views about our principles and policies; they do not plan to return to serve the country. But they do not yet belong to the group of people who actively participate in activities against our government. . . .

D. Fourth category: These are activists who have participated in the antigovernment movement. We must conduct criticism, education, and necessary reasoned struggles against these people, adopting the policy of dividing and splitting them. . .

E. Fifth category: These are reactionary core elements who actively organize and plan antigovernment activities. They are the targets for us to expose and strike at. . . .[51]

The document estimates that less than 5 percent of all overseas Chinese students and scholars fall into the first category. The fourth category contains about 10 percent, and the fifth category is composed of about one hundred persons. In addition, the document lists the names of several leaders of the prodemocracy movement.[52]

It is reasonable to think that the Chinese leadership would be able to formulate this type of analysis only if it possessed accurate information about the structure, composition, and activities of various overseas Chinese dissident groups. The documents (plus Xu Lin's testimony) confirm press reports of intelligence activities against prodemocracy activists. In the aggregate, this evidence indicates that the Chinese government actively exploits its intelligence services and other embassy units to harass, intimidate, subvert, and control overseas dissident groups as well as to collect information regarding them.

In several interviews, prodemocracy dissidents and a defector formerly employed by the Ministry of Foreign Affairs identified Zhao Xixin, Li Jingchun, and Ni Mengxiong as the three individuals in the Chinese embassy in Washington responsible for implementing the harassment campaign. Minister Zhao is reportedly an MSS officer and chief of espionage operations conducted in the United States. Minister-Consular Li coordinates espionage and surveillance of students as well as harassment activities conducted by the educational affairs department.[53]

Yu Zhaoji, first secretary, is responsible for compiling the information acquired by the education department's collection efforts. In addition, Xu Lin credits first secretaries Wang Zurong and Xia Yingqi for being remarkably effective in monitoring and intimidating Chinese student dissidents. Wang was particularly active at the University of Maryland.[54]

But in 1991 his effectiveness was dramatically reduced after some Maryland students recorded his telephoned threats. The university's Chinese student association voted to terminate all contact between its members and Wang.[55]

Another education department employee, Wang Weiji, was also quite active against student dissidents. He subsequently defected to the United States, but there appears to be some question as to the validity of his defection. While working at the embassy, Wang confided to close colleagues that he was an MSS officer. He traveled around the United States by himself, a privilege reserved for intelligence and security personnel; and he frequently exceeded the standard per diem allowance, a practice that caused bureaucratic problems when the education department asked the MSS to cover the additional expenditures. Wang's defection may be an MSS provocation designed to gather information on American counterintelligence methodology. The U.S. government has broken off its relationship with Wang. His wife returned to the PRC, and he currently works at a Chinese restaurant in Washington, D.C.[56]

The actions of embassy personnel and the policy guidance they have received show that the apparent objective of the Beijing leadership is to resist political change. That resistance requires employing all elements of the government structure to control overseas dissidents. Considering the information requirements behind the military campaigns of suppression in Tibet (1986-87), Beijing (1989), and Xinjiang Province (1990), one can conclude that in the immediate future China will dedicate a considerable portion of its intelligence resources toward internal dissidents.

Chapter 6

Domestic Operations

To describe the nature and scope of domestic MSS activities accurately, it is first necessary to review its operational climate. At first glance, the intelligence and security environment in the PRC may appear to be relatively benign. The only categories of people who routinely report surveillance or other forms of harassment are dissidents and foreign journalists. The average tourist, academic, or businessman visiting China does not immediately notice surveillance or overt intelligence collection activities. However, an internal security structure that collects information for the CPC is woven into the fabric of Chinese society as well as into its economic, cultural, and political infrastructure.

The fundamental building block in domestic intelligence is the work unit (*danwei*). These units exist in all places of employment, communes, and schools. They are designed to promulgate CPC policies down to the lowest levels of society, and they work closely with the MSS. The units and committees are headed by CPC cadres and comprise the workers or residents of a specific area. Most *danwei* (depending on their size) are divided into personnel, administrative, and security subsections. Residential areas also have neighborhood committees, which serve the same function. Each *danwei* or neighborhood committee maintains dossiers on its membership, including such information as work and family history, education, travel history (in China and overseas), and political and ideological correctness. Depending on its size, each unit also reviews travel plans and allocates housing, school, and work assignments to its members. Accusations and other evidence concerning an individual's loyalty to the CPC are included in one's file.[1]

With the *danwei* and neighborhood committees CPC cadres have the means to coerce members to inform on each other. Members do not have the option of refusing to cooperate. The use of danwei, combined with the information collection operations of law enforcement and intelligence agencies, allows for effective monitoring of activities that are considered threatening by the CPC. The case of an American scholar conducting research at the Central China Normal Institute in Wuhan offers a good example of how a *danwei* can be used to monitor foreigners. The scholar, Michael Gasster, was visited by New York Times reporter Fox Butterfield. Moments after Butterfield's arrival at Gasster's residence the head of the school danwei called to ask about the identity of the visitor and purpose of the visit. Someone in the danwei had noticed the presence of a stranger and reported it to the security section. Gasster later told the reporter that the danwei constantly monitored all his activities.[2]

In addition to party committees, Chinese intelligence services can count on state ministries, people's friendship societies, academic institutions, and the military-industrial complex to support activities such as agent recruitment and information collection as well as to provide cover jobs to their operatives. All of the information developed by the intelligence process is forwarded to the party. For example, if an academic institution entertains a foreign scholar, information about that individual is passed to the party's provincial-level Political Legal Leading Committee (PLLC).[3]

This process ensures that the party will retain its control of information. Another aspect of the PRC's internal collection network that adds to the perception of a benign security environment is the aggressive use of technical surveillance measures. Many of the prominent hotels that cater to foreigners are equipped for the technical surveillance of guests and visitors. In May 1989 Chinese student dissident Wuer Kaixi was recorded on videotape as he ate lunch with foreign journalists in the Beijing Hotel. The tape was made by the hotel's static surveillance cameras, located in the ceiling of the dining room. Other prominent Beijing hotels that are known to monitor the activities of their clientele are the Palace Hotel, the Great Wall Hotel, and the Xiang Shan Hotel.[4]

In addition, the MPS owns the Kunlun Hotel and probably monitors its guests.[5]

According to Chinese prostitutes who frequent the Jianguo Hotel, the guest rooms used by foreign businessmen there also contain microphones.[6]

The Palace Hotel is owned in part by the PLA's general staff department. One of the American contractors for the Xiang Shan Hotel had a series of verbal battles with PRC officials as it was being built.[7] The Chinese demanded that additional wires be installed in each room. The purpose of the wires was to tie in microphones.[8]

It is logical to expect that the technical surveillance of foreigners in these and other Chinese hotels is carried out by the MSS's technical operations department (see chapter 4). Another, more obvious use of technical collection techniques can be seen on Beijing streetcorners. Video cameras positioned atop streetlights ostensibly are there to observe traffic.[9] However, they could be used just as easily to augment the information collected by MSS physical surveillance teams. For example, the MSS might want to determine the daily movement patterns of foreign journalists and diplomats. This task could be accomplished in part if street surveillance cameras recorded a diplomat's or foreign journalist's vehicle (which can be identified by its distinctive license plates) traveling a certain route on a particular day of the week. It is not known, however, what PRC agency is responsible for extracting information of intelligence value from these street cameras. The use of these systems to identify protesters shortly after the violence at Tiananmen Square suggests that responsibility belongs to the MPS. The fact that traffic control is a function of the MPS supports this thesis.[10]

Technical surveillance in the PRC is conducted by several agencies. For example, the monitoring of diplomatic, military, and international communications that involve foreign nationals is conducted by the Third Department of the PLA's general staff department.[11]

This department is responsible for signals and communications intelligence and is considerably larger than all other elements of the PRC's intelligence apparatus.[12]

The video and audio surveillance of foreigners in China is the responsibility of the MSS. Considering the amount of resources involved, it is likely that this function is executed with support from the investigations department of the MPS. The monitoring of international mail and telecommunications that involve Chinese nationals is handled by the Ministry of Post and Telecommunications at provincial monitoring stations. As of 1985 an average of 26 percent of international mail was intercepted and screened by the ministry.[13]

Presumably, given Beijing's increased security concerns, today's percentage is considerably higher. In addition to these forms of technical intelligence collection, the MSS is becoming more active in domestic HUMINT operations. The domestic or internal responsibilities of the MSS appear to focus on penetrating foreign intelligence services, recruiting agents for domestic and overseas espionage, investigating foreign espionage, and collecting information on counterrevolutionary activities. Domestic intelligence operations are directed at China's foreign population and Chinese citizens with foreign or dissident contacts. These operations are conducted by the internal bureau of the MSS, in some cases with the assistance of the investigations bureau of the MPS.[14]

A study of China's police and security agencies is beyond the scope of this work. But insofar as intelligence collection and production is concerned, the MSS and MPS acquire information, analyze it, and disseminate finished intelligence to support the information requirements of Chinese policymakers. Unlike the MSS, the MPS has as its primary role the physical security of the nation. It is charged with supervising the operations of all local police forces, civilian security functions (airport, railroad, and industrial security, as well as customs), and the People's Armed Police (PAP).[15]

The MPS's authority over the PAP appears to be only administrative, since it has not been able to exercise control over the activities of the force outside the Beijing area.[16]

The PAP is responsive to the party's central military commission; however, its budget is controlled by the state council through the MPS.[17]

It is probable that the MPS will exert an increasing degree of control over the PAP.

The MSS is primarily an intelligence agency, but — like the FBI in the United States — it affects police functions as well. It also conducts other functions such as hearings that are controlled by the judiciary in Western democracies. Therefore, the MSS has a wide scope of authority in domestic intelligence activities, authority that overlaps into the law enforcement responsibilities of the MPS. The MSS is "authorized to exercise powers granted to public security institutions by the Constitution and laws, to wit, investigation, detention and arrest of criminals, and the holding of preliminary hearings."[18]

As such, it maintains a close working relationship with the police and security elements of the MPS.

Political repression is not a new phenomenon in the PRC. Many of the MSS's domestic intelligence functions involve the suppression of all forms of internal dissent. Secessionist movements in Tibet (Xizang) and the predominantly Muslim Xinjiang province, as well as urban-based prodemocracy activities, are the main concerns of Beijing's leadership.

Since the 1989 Tiananmen Square protests, repressive police and military measures have been applied with renewed vigor against China's academics, minorities, and some urban workers. Tactical intelligence is necessary to support police and military actions against these targets in an effort to identify and neutralize the efforts of persons who the Beijing leadership defines as counterrevolutionaries. Organized prodemocracy advocates and ethnic or regional independence movements are likely to be priority targets for intelligence collection activities. Officials who represent countries seen as sympathetic to these causes for religious, ethnic, political, or ideological reasons, are also likely to receive more attention.

In recent years Chinese policymakers have publicly blamed internal dissension on foreign influence. They charge the West, and particularly the United States, with attempting to foment political change through a process of engagement and "peaceful evolution." In internal publications CPC cadres are warned of the disastrous economic effects of "peaceful evolution" on Communist party members in the former Soviet Union.[19]

As discussed above (see chapter 5), information about "America's campaign of peaceful evolution" has been high on the list of PRC intelligence collection priorities since 1989. This practice of blaming foreign influence for internal problems has a long tradition in Chinese politics, dating back at least to the mid-1800s.

The ill effect of foreign influence is a realistic fear from the perspective of the current PRC leadership. This may be due in part to the tight control of information that is so much a part of Chinese society. As the country has opened up to the world, its citizens have gained exposure to the Western concepts of inalienable human rights, freedom, and democracy. Recently this exposure has increased to significant levels in academic, governmental, and industrial sectors.

This has caused a degree of disenchantment with China's Communist political system, manifested in the prodemocracy dissident movement. Compounding this difficulty is the substantial increase in the PRC's postal and telecommunications ties to the outside world. These further weaken the party's ability to restrict the flow of information.

The Beijing leadership has instituted a multiagency, coordinated effort to collect intelligence and conduct law enforcement and military operations in an attempt to quell internal dissent. Nowhere is this effort more evident than in the Tibet Autonomous Region (TAR). Intelligence operations and direct applications of force intended to suppress the Tibetan independence movement are coordinated by the party's Xizhang Province Special Working Group.[20]

The PRC's attempts to keep the Tibetan population in line includes information collection activities conducted by the MSS, MPS, Central Department of the United Front (United Front Works Department), Central Commission for State Nationalities' Affairs, State Bureau for Religious Affairs, Central Commission for Discipline Inspection, State Bureau for the Protection of Cultural Antiquities, and State Bureau for Commodity Inspection.[21]

On 4 March 1986 the CPC's central administrative unit sent a cable to the working group in Tibet containing policy directives from Party Secretary Zhao Ziyang and President Yang Shangkun. Regarding intelligence, the cable included the following guidance:

1   The Armed Police to prepare for full-scale combat. Should watch closely the development of the situation and report back details as they occur. . . .
2.   Border troops to go on full alert. All Indian army movements to be monitored. Any border movements to be reported.
3.   Journalists from the mainland to Tibet to be told that reporting the uprising is banned. Those who violate this instruction can be dealt with on the spot.
4.   Close watch to be placed on the movements at the consulate or trade offices of neighboring countries India, Nepal, Bhutan, and Sikkim. No action to be taken without reporting to the State Security Ministry.
5.   Any foreign journalists found in Tibet to be investigated closely. Should be transferred to the working group sent by the State Security Bureau.[22]

It is interesting to note that this document orders elements of the MPS to monitor the movements of diplomatic and trade personnel from neighboring states but prohibits any action until after the MSS is consulted. Equal concern is expressed about the presence of foreign journalists – while other security agencies are involved, primary responsibility is reserved for the MSS. It is also noteworthy that border troops are told to monitor the movements of the Indian army. These units are under the command of regional as opposed to strategic military forces. Reconnaissance units are subelements of the border troops.

Interviews of Tibetan refugees in the summer of 1992 revealed that most had at least peripheral knowledge of, or believed in the existence of, some type of informant network in the TAR run by the Chinese government. In several cases individuals admitted to giving information to the MPS's local public security bureau under torture or the threat of torture.[23]

The MPS was well known for deploying agents in support of the PRC's efforts to subjugate Tibet. Neither the MSS nor the PLA were ever mentioned as forces involved in recruiting or running agents. This indicates that the MSS is not as involved as the MPS in keeping agents among the general population. This contention is supported by the central committee document quoted above, which clearly designates the MSS as responsible for monitoring foreign officials and journalists in Tibet.

MPS operators tended to recruit agents who "were normally poor, uneducated people who were not considered a threat to the Communists."[24]

Intimidation of the prospective agent is the agency's primary tool, often combined with the actual imprisonment of and physical violence to the agent and his or her family. Recruitment targets were also selected based on their access and ability to satisfy information requirements. They were always ethnic Tibetans.[25]

In Tibet the MPS appears to concentrate primarily on developing large numbers of low-level agents. Usually, recruited agents are not told to pursue specific information requirements and are not trained in espionage tradecraft. There are reportedly no standard procedures for OPSEC or clandestine communications. The use of several agents to go after a particular target is normal practice, as is asking agents to report on the activities of other agents.[26]

The validity of the data collected must therefore be determined by comparing multiple source reports.

The MPS's recruitment and handling of sensitive or high-level agents differs from that of its comparatively low-level sources. In one case in March 1990 a prospective agent was lured from Tibet to Chengdu on the pretext of a deal to purchase photographic equipment. While in Chengdu he was arrested and detained at a hotel normally reserved for party cadres. The source believes that his recruitment took place in Chengdu because of the "high profile" of his family in Lhasa. Presumably, if he had been arrested in Lhasa he would have become suspected as an MPS informer – and his arrest would have pointed to the existence of a broader MPS investigation.[27]

After his arrest in Chengdu this individual was taken to the local office of the PAP. After several days of interrogations and threats, the source agreed to cooperate by reporting the activities of family members suspected of involvement with the resistance in the TAR. His information objectives were quite specific and prioritized. Afterward the source was offered communications equipment as well as financial and personnel support. Arrangements were made for a covert meeting with a handler in the TAR.[28]

Analysis of the source's description of his arrest, interrogation, and subsequent recruitment reveals some interesting operational characteristics. First, the MPS had identified the source through an individual at his workplace. This person made the travel and lodging arrangements and accompanied the source on the trip. Second, the recruitment effort was coordinated by the MPS, PAP, and party cadres from Chengdu and the TAR. One of the intelligence officers who the recruit met in Chengdu – Teching Gyaltso – was designated as his point of contact in the TAR.[29]

Third, the source was told specifically what information to collect.

Fourth, the recruit received technical and financial support. Finally, a secret method of communication was put in place before the agent was deployed.

Other cases of MPS collection activities in Tibet also highlight a limited capability to conduct sophisticated operations. In several instances, agents reportedly passed information to their MPS handler in the form of written reports. The handler ran five to ten agents at a time and occasionally made substantive changes in the contents of their reports. Records maintained by the MPS on sensitive or high-level agents ascribe an alphanumeric code to the individual and include descriptions of his or her operational activities, travel expenses, and reimbursement.[30]

Outside Tibet, other operations supported by tactical intelligence involve the identification and apprehension of prodemocracy advocates. The MSS has a relatively good record in penetrating and neutralizing underground organizations that advocate democratic change in China. Most of this success appears to have come at the regional and local levels – but the number of arrests of dissidents at these low levels has decimated the ability of prodemocracy groups to organize nationally. Regional intelligence efforts have proven accurate and timely enough to identify many dissident groups in their infancy. The case of the Shanghai-based prodemocracy group Lutan (Forum) serves as an example of this capability. Despite the use of security measures such as code names and facsimile machines, the group was detected, identified, and neutralized before it could issue its first publication.[31]

One reason that the MSS and MPS have had a degree of success against prodemocracy activists is the dissidents' limited geographic range. Throughout the 1980s and early 1990s China's prodemocracy movement has been led by intellectuals and supported by urban workers. Its general area of operations has therefore been limited to universities and factories in the cities. The resources of the MSS would be spread thin if dissidents were able to organize outside the urban environment.

In contrast to their performance at the local level, the MSS and MPS have not effectively produced and used intelligence to attack pro-democracy activists nationwide. The flow of intelligence between MSS and MPS offices in different provinces and municipalities is so limited that it severely hampers police and military actions. This is largely why the PRC failed to prevent the flight of many prodemocracy leadership figures in the wake of Tiananmen. In 1989 a dissident group in Hong Kong developed a clandestine intelligence network to locate democracy activists and help them escape. Among those the network was able to "exfiltrate" were six of China's most wanted students, including Li Lu, Wuer Kaixi, and Chai Ling; two senior government reformers, Chen Yizi and Yan Jiaqi; and one of the movement's leading intellectuals, Su Xiaokang. The Hong Kong-based organization used front companies, false documents, and disguises to aid the fugitives.[32]

This group was able to send teams into China on at least five occasions. They located the fugitives in several towns, municipalities, and provinces before PRC authorities were able to do so, shuttling them from province to province before escaping to Hong Kong. On only one occasion was PRC intelligence able to detect the covert rescue operation. This was allegedly due to information received from an MSS source and resulted in the arrests of prodemocracy dissidents Chen Zeming and Wang Juntao and Hong Kong businessman Lu Haixing.[33]

The MPS and New China News Agency actively collect information about prodemocracy activists in Hong Kong. "We are accumulating information about people who are against the Chinese government," stated Tao Siju, minister of public security. "The NCNA has its own methods and channels to collect information, and we have our own. The emphases are different."[34]

Zhou Nan, director of the NCNA's Hong Kong branch, said that his agency "collects only newspaper clippings, information on Hong Kong affairs advisers, and who's who."[35] Given the agency's history as a cover organization for MSS operations (see Chapter 5), it is likely that the MSS is actively working under NCNA cover against prodemocracy advocates in Hong Kong and Macao.

The failure of the MSS and MPS to detect and neutralize the Hong Kong organization earlier illuminates some functional limitations of the PRC's intelligence collection capabilities. One handicap is caused by the CPC's pervasive presence throughout the intelligence structure. The linear movement of information throughout the PRC intelligence apparatus – indeed, the entire government – is intended to keep the party informed and in control at all levels. Information developed by one agency must by relayed to the party apparatus before it can be disseminated to the working levels of another government agency. It is apparent that this pattern does not facilitate timely communication between various municipal and provincial intelligence bodies. This shortcoming allowed fugitives with forged documents to move between provinces with relative impunity.

The inability of intelligence services outside a single province or municipality to share information in a timely manner without involving the CPC may be the most identifiable flaw in the effectiveness of the PRC's domestic intelligence and security structure. To avoid capture, prodemocracy activists should therefore decentralize their operations over several provinces to take advantage of this weakness.

Another weakness of the PRC's intelligence apparatus is corruption. CPC documents, press reports, and student protesters at Tiananmen square all recognized that corruption is pervasive throughout the Chinese government. There is nothing to suggest that the intelligence and security services are immune to such influences in their ranks. In fact, corrupt (or sympathetic) intelligence, police, and army officers helped extract dissidents from the PRC.[36]

Domestic intelligence activities are by no means directed only at internal dissidents. The growing number of Westerners traveling to China each year, combined with Beijing's fear of Western influences, has resulted in an increase in the amount of intelligence resources devoted to domestic surveillance operations. Foreign journalists in China frequently report harassment, recruitment attempts, and intensive surveillance.[37]

Another aspect of the intelligence activities directed against foreign journalists is the government's intimidation of PRC nationals. Chinese citizens are often detained or questioned after they talk to Western reporters. The punishment for talking to a journalist can range from garnishment of wages to prison time.[38] Some period of interrogation appears to be the norm. The MSS reportedly conducts surveillance on foreign journalists by foot, bicycle, motorcycle, and automobile. MSS teams on foot sometimes use radios.[39]

The British Broadcasting Corporation (BBC) maintains a list of the license tags of known surveillance vehicles. Information booklets about foreign journalists are produced by the ministry and distributed to provincial foreign affairs bureaus. These publications rate reporters and their attitude toward China as perceived by Beijing. The provincial bureaus use this data to decide whether to allow a journalist to enter a particular region.[40]

Other means used to monitor and control the foreign media involve forcing journalists to live together in designated housing compounds. These are guarded by members of the PAP, who probably record comings and goings of residents and visitors. Some of the compounds are watched by video cameras. In at least one compound, video monitoring devices were discovered hidden in the ceilings of elevators. Eavesdropping on the home and work telephones of foreign journalists is routine.[41]

Lastly, the Chinese workers in the compounds are provided by the Ministry of Foreign Affairs's Diplomatic Services Bureau (DSB) and report on the daily activities of the reporters.[42]

The level of resources that the MSS has dedicated to monitoring the activities of foreign journalists indicates a high counterintelligence priority. The MSS's actions – intensive technical and physical surveillance, harassment, and attempted recruitment – are designed not to develop positive intelligence, but primarily to neutralize the activities of these reporters. The logical inference is that, for whatever reason, Beijing policymakers feel threatened by the foreign media, over which they have no direct control.

This fear of foreign influence is due in part to the fact that the control of information has always been an important element in the CPC's maintenance of power. Manipulation of information for public consumption, or propaganda, is not considered an intelligence function by the CPC policy apparatus. Whereas by Western standards propaganda is considered a form of covert action, in the PRC it is a normal function of government. The Chinese government's use of propaganda is so pervasive that even internal *neibu* documents such as the NCNA's Reference News are manipulated to support the CPC.[43]

The intensive intelligence effort directed at foreign journalists reveals a great deal about the capabilities and intentions of the MSS's internal bureau. One question that must be asked is why reporters are routinely able to detect the ministry's surveillance efforts. Presumably the personnel assigned to this task are seasoned professionals and should be able to avoid detection. There are two reasonable explanations: (1) the MSS wants to intimidate foreign journalists, or (2) the MSS has increased its surveillance staff in recent years and has been unable to train and deploy them properly. The available evidence is too sketchy to support either conclusion at this point. However, Chinese leaders have recently made public pronouncements calling for increased security measures and vigilance against foreign spies.[44]

The MSS's most important domestic operations are those directed against the diplomatic community in the PRC. These activities encompass both counterintelligence investigations and positive intelligence recruitment operations (see chapter 4). The attempted recruitment of a U.S. diplomatic communications officer in Beijing in 1988 is clear evidence that the MSS actively targets other nations' diplomats.

In addition to outright recruitment attempts, the MSS has tried to use electronics to penetrate the American embassy in Beijing and the consulate in Shanghai. In 1985 the MSS recovered construction blueprints from a trash container in the embassy. Although unclassified, the blueprints could easily be used to determine the best locations for technical penetrations, provided one had physical access to the target area. The MSS considered the information so valuable that the female intelligence officer responsible for the operation received an achievement award.[45]

Another incident of covert technical penetration became public in May 1987 when a U.S. State Department diplomatic security officer reportedly discovered electronic listening devices in the Beijing embassy and the Shanghai consulate. This revelation was followed by the discovery of underground tunnels in both facilities.[46]

If detecting the devices led investigators to the tunnels, then they must have used wires as opposed to transmitters. This means that the MSS or one of its agents must have had physical access to the buildings over a sufficiently long period to plant microphones and connect them to a nearby listening post. Hard-wired listening devices require significantly more time on target than do those that send signals via transmitters.

Another means of monitoring foreign diplomats is through Chinese nationals employed as clerks, nannies, maids, and chauffeurs. The foreign community in the PRC – diplomats, journalists, and business representatives alike – hires such workers from the DSB.[47]

These individuals are required to report the daily activities of their employers.[48] In addition, MSS case officers assume cover jobs in the DSB to coordinate the collection activities of these workers and to monitor their relationships with foreign nationals.[49]

Through DSB-affiliated Chinese workers, danwei, MSS agent recruitment operations, and technical and physical surveillance, it appears that the PRC maintains a close watch over foreign diplomats. According to an MSS publication, "Foreign diplomats are open spies . . . [and] have used a thousand means, including bribes and sex, to recruit agents, including more than ten of our government staff."[50]

The portrayal of all foreign diplomats as "open spies" is partly attributable to the fact that China's leadership, as well as its security apparatus, views all foreigners with suspicion. Beijing exhibits what might be described in Western terms as a paranoiac fear of foreign influence. One can only speculate about the root cause of this mind-set. However, the desire to maintain political power in a changing ideological and economic environment is likely to be one element.

The fears of Beijing policymakers ultimately result in a nationwide internal control structure in which massive intelligence resources are deployed against Chinese nationals as well as foreign diplomats, journalists, academics, and businesspersons. China's intelligence services, however, perceive these individuals as more than threats. Individuals in each category represent potentially lucrative sources of information, technology, and other materials to support China's political, diplomatic, economic, and military needs.

Chapter 7

Agent Recruitment Methods

The MSS prefers to recruit agents in China. Recruiting foreign nationals on one's own soil tends to be a secure and cost-effective method of conducting espionage. The primary benefits are the safe environment for the case officer and the lack of ramifications should the prospective agent decline the recruitment pitch. Chinese intelligence and security services regularly use this approach to recruiting espionage assets and agents of influence. Potential agents are sought in all clusters of visiting foreigners. For the most part, MSS recruitment methods tend to be crude by the standards of Western intelligence services. For example, several Westerners who spent time in PRC prisons reported offers of freedom in return for promising to act on behalf of the PRC back home.[1]

A secondary benefit of recruiting espionage agents in one's own country is that governments need not incur the cost of maintaining case officers and their families overseas. In addition, this method is generally considered safe vis-a-vis foreign counterintelligence concerns. Because the MSS monitors diplomats in China so diligently, there is less opportunity for foreign intelligence services to target and recruit Chinese officials. Hostile services are also less likely to send their agents provocateurs to the PRC because of the personal risk involved.

In China recruitment operations against foreign nationals include diplomats and government officials as targets as well as academics, journalists, and businesspersons. The MSS recruits these people to conduct espionage against their home government, to influence events overseas on behalf of the PRC, or to provide business intelligence and restricted technology. The MSS and China's Military Intelligence Department (MID) invite foreign scholars to lecture or attend conferences in the PRC under the guise of research associations or univer-

58

sities. All expenses for the visiting lecturer and his or her family frequently are paid for by the intelligence services. The visiting specialist is subjected to a demanding itinerary of lectures, meetings, travel, and social engagements. The purpose of this rigorous schedule is to wear down the prospective recruit's physical and mental stamina. The visitor is encouraged to partake of alcohol as much as circumstances permit. The subject is then more approachable concerning personal or confidential matters.[2]

Academics and other subject-matter experts are potentially lucrative targets for the PRC intelligence services for two reasons: (1) they possess unique insights in fields of interest to the MSS or MID, and (2) they have access to policymakers and other potential recruitment targets. In the first scenario, less subtlety is required to solicit information because the individual came to China expecting to provide details on a specific subject. The second scenario necessitates a more discrete approach. Another intelligence objective achieved by hosting foreign scholars is to persuade and co-opt those who are in positions to influence policymakers in their home countries.[3]

In addition to sponsoring short-term lecture tours, the PRC intelligence apparatus targets visiting scholars participating in university exchange programs. For example, in the late 1980s American professor Larry Engelmann taught at a center established at Nanjing University by John Hopkins University. One of Engelmann's students, Xu Maihong, apparently fell in love with him and confessed that she and several other students were PLA intelligence officers. Their responsibilities were to learn English and to keep track of the activities of American scholars and students, in preparation for assignment overseas. She told Engelmann that all incoming mail was reviewed and that the PLA monitored the telephone conversations of the resident American professors.[4]

For the most part, MSS attempts to recruit foreign journalists living in China are as simplistic as its operations against visiting scholars. For example, many reporters have been offered classified information over the phone.[5]

This approach was used in February 1992 against *Times* of London journalist Catherine Sampson:

> I recently met a man who claimed to be an army officer. "My nephew wants to go abroad to study," he said, "and his mother asked me to help him get a little money together. I thought,

how can I, a simple army officer, make money? And then I thought to myself, I know, I can make a little money by selling state secrets. Would you like to buy some army documents?" It was not clear to me whether he was a simpleminded bureau officer or just plain simpleminded.[6]

As intelligence recruitment attempts go, offering classified information over the telephone is a transparent instance of entrapment designed so that when the unsuspecting victim goes to pick up the material he or she is arrested. The individual is then offered an opportunity to cooperate with the intelligence service rather than face prosecution for espionage. If the victim does not have diplomatic immunity (as is the case with journalists and businesspersons), there is considerable pressure to cooperate. Generally the individual is made to sign an agreement to ensure continued cooperation at a future date.

Another frequently used and equally crude recruitment method used by the MSS involves sexual entrapments. Male foreign journalists in China routinely receive calls from Chinese women who express a passionate, seemingly uncontrollable desire to meet them.[7]

The goal is to lure individuals into sexual relationships that are subsequently exploited by the MSS. Victims are either blackmailed, if they are married or prohibited by their employer from having contact with PRC nationals, or gradually manipulated into providing more and more information. As simple as this ploy appears, Chinese intelligence services have used it to achieve several notable successes.

While stationed in Beijing in 1964, French diplomat Bernard Boursicot became involved in a sexual relationship with Chinese opera singer Shi Peipu. The CPC investigations department exploited this relationship and recruited Boursicot as an espionage agent in 1969.[8] In return, he was allowed to marry Shi Peipu and to leave China. Boursicot remained a productive agent for the PRC until 1985, when he and his wife were arrested by French security officials. During the trial, France's National Surete revealed that Shi was not a woman but a man — a transvestite. Given the unusual nature of this case (which was the basis for a recent Broadway play, Madam Butterfly), it is important to note the intensive research and overall effort expended by the CPC investigations department to identify, assess, and finally recruit Boursicot.

In 1988 the MSS tried to recruit a U.S. State Department communications officer who was involved in sexual relationship with a female Chinese national.[9] It is not known whether the MSS orchestrated the relationship or just sought to exploit it; in any event, the woman tried to blackmail him into spying for the PRC.[10] The attempt was unsuccessful because the American target reported the recruitment pitch to the embassy security officer. The individual was subsequently recalled to the United States. Although the MSS was unsuccessful in recruiting this particular asset, it probably exploited the ongoing relationship to gather data on the personnel and operating procedures of the American embassy.

The MSS appears to be far more comfortable recruiting persons of Chinese descent as opposed to non-Chinese foreign nationals. But one must consider that Beijing expects ethnically Chinese foreign nationals to have some loyalty to China. As a result, espionage recruitment techniques used against such persons in some ways resemble those used against Chinese nationals.

The MSS uses two main themes in recruiting foreign nationals of Chinese ancestry. First, it appeals to their perceived obligation to help the land of their heritage, thereby exploiting sentimental feelings of ethnic pride. Second, it implies that family members still in the PRC will receive unfavorable treatment unless the subjects cooperate. The latter approach is quite stressful for the subjects and a strong motivational factor in favor of compliance.

The theme of helping China recurs in a number of recruitment attempts of foreign-born and mainland Chinese.[11] In the early 1980s a Union Carbide official and U.S. citizen of Chinese descent who was working in Beijing was asked to provide company secrets in order to "help China," as well as for personal profit.[12] The offer was rejected; however, the same pitch was used successfully on Larry Chin.

The use of the "help China" recruitment approach has worked for other intelligence services besides the MSS. The former Soviet KGB adopted this recruitment method to manipulate persons of Chinese descent into conducting espionage against the PRC. The pitch was modified to convince the source that he or she would help the Chinese people, as opposed to the PRC government.[13]

Or else prospective agents would be persuaded that their cooperation would enhance China's relations with the Soviet Union. What little success the Soviets enjoyed against the PRC was attributable to these recruitment techniques.

The MSS holds a considerable advantage in recruiting foreign nationals with relatives in China. The prospect of retaliation or favorable treatment of family members there is always present. The threat of actions against family members is used routinely to pressure Chinese nationals overseas into working for the ministry. This can be seen in the threats directed at prodemocracy activists and in the case of Larry Wu-tai Chin.[14]

Chin admitted to giving the MPS biographical information on CIA co-worker Victoria Loo. His stated objective was to assist the PRC in locating Loo's brother in China so that he could be used to recruit the CIA employee.[15]

The MSS uses a number of techniques to recruit, train, and deploy PRC nationals traveling abroad to conduct clandestine espionage operations. This practice was revealed in the cases of a number of Chinese scholars and students recruited as low-level agents. The recruits are divided into two categories: long-term agents and short-term agents.[16]

Long-term agents are referred to in MSS slang as "fish at the bottom of the ocean" (*Chun di eu*).[17] These are individuals recruited as espionage agents who will not be activated until a later date. The following narrative describes the recruitment and deployment of one such agent.

A PRC national was recruited as a low-level agent by provincial MSS officials. The source had two academic degrees in the hard sciences. The recruitment process started approximately six months before the prospective agent was to travel to the United States for advanced graduate studies. The individual was approached by the leader of his work unit (*danwei*), who told him that two persons from the province's foreign affairs bureau had come to see him.[18]

The first interview lasted about one hour and involved a general discussion of the source's proposed course of study overseas. The officials emphasized that his plans were all in order and that they were concerned merely for the well-being of all students traveling to the West. They offered assistance if any administrative problems arose. The officials stressed that they were aware he was a good scholar and had an outgoing personality.

Several weeks later the source was summoned (via telephone) by the same officials to an office in the city. The office had no outside identification signs. During a two-hour discussion the representatives again said that they were concerned for his welfare and just wanted to make sure his preparations for study abroad were going well. They also reminded him to "remember your family, the Communist party, and our country" while overseas. The prospective agent was encouraged to do well in his academic program and to make all the high-level contacts that he could. Foreign knowledge was very beneficial to China. They told him of several famous Chinese scientists who returned to the PRC after their time abroad, including astrophysicist Chien Hsuehshen. (Chien was a colonel in the U.S. Army during World War II. During the 1950s he was investigated for having belonged to the Communist party in 1939. He returned to China to launch its space program.)

The officials asked to be notified once the source was sure which American university he would be attending (he was awaiting the results of his scholarship applications). After the second interview, the source became somewhat suspicious of the motives of these "foreign affairs bureau" representatives. Based on what the officials had told him about their academic backgrounds, the source subsequently located and talked to some of their former colleagues and classmates. Several individuals identified the representatives as provincial MSS employees.

When the source received a scholarship he notified the officials, as directed, and was summoned for a third discussion. They asked if all his plans were falling into place without complications and if there was anything they could do to help. On this occasion the source was asked to share his opinions about China, the Communist party, and the Tiananmen incident. The source responded positively to all these inquiries, for fear of being denied permission to travel. A fourth meeting was then scheduled: a two-week training session in Beijing.

This session was held less than two months before the source was to leave for the United States. He stayed at the MSS's Beijing guest house, and his primary contact was identified only as "Mr. Xu." Due to time constraints, the source was able to attend just one week of lectures. The MSS representatives were quite flexible about the schedule and told him that the lectures were meant to "help you understand America." Course content was a combination of facts about life in the United States, the benefits of Chinese communism and cooperation, and personal security practices to use while abroad.

The first series of lectures dealt with the American media. Instructors identified organizations that owned newspapers and magazines, and how that ownership influenced the conservative or liberal positions of those publications. Specific media personalities were also identified as either liberal or conservative. The source felt that these lectures were an accurate portrayal of the American media.

The second series of lectures was about various Chinese student organizations in the United States. The dissident groups were all categorized as an antigovernment threat; the students who belonged to these organizations had turned against communism and had "no future." The source was instructed to show a polite level of interest in prodemocracy organizations but not to become overly involved. MSS personnel suggested using the excuse of having to study to avoid being drawn into dissident activities. The source was cautioned not to attend antigovernment rallies.

The third series of lectures was about the American political process. Topics included the foundations of the multiparty system, the sources of political power, and the prevalence of corruption in America. The source felt these lectures were somewhat jaundiced but generally presented an accurate view of American politics. The final lectures concerned short- and long-term intelligence objectives, personal behavior, communications, security concerns, and emergency contact instructions. In addition, at the end of the day the source was told about the MSS's career and retirement benefits.

The method by which this source was recruited, as well as the information presented in the lectures, is noteworthy for our purposes. The MSS officers told the agent that he was picked because he was both academically superior and socially outgoing. They valued these qualities in the source in contrast to students who "have only book knowledge." The agent was encouraged to use every opportunity to meet people who were (or might become) influential. These statements strongly indicate that their objective was to develop a long-term agent who could penetrate deep into the target environment.

Although the MSS encouraged the source to develop contacts, academic achievement was always stressed as an equal priority. He was told that just gaining knowledge from foreign study and exposure was a significant achievement and would benefit China. The intelligence officers warned the agent that some other students before him had "behaved poorly." They had betrayed China by reporting their clandestine relationship with the MSS to the U.S. government. Like the prodemocracy dissidents, they were said to have no future in the PRC. The agent was further instructed not to tell anyone of his covert relationship with the Chinese government. Officials emphasized that their primary concern was for the agent's safety, and that no piece of information was ever important enough to put an agent at risk. Not telling anyone about this clandestine arrangement would ensure the safety of everyone involved.

On arrival at his college in the United States, the agent was instructed to send a letter of confirmation to an accommodation address in his home province. Thereafter, he was to mail a letter to that address once every three months. Each was supposed to contain information about his physical well-being and financial status. In addition, he was required to send notice if he decided to change to a different academic major.

In case of emergency the agent was told to call one of two phone numbers in his home province. The numbers were associated with the provincial office of the Commission of Science, Technology, and Industry for National Defense (COSTIND). The officers cautioned that the Americans would be able to determine the location of the PRC contact as well as the contents of the conversation. Only in the case of a life-threatening emergency was the agent to contact the Chinese embassy in Washington, D.C.

The MSS officers advised the agent that while he was gone they would take care of his family. On several Chinese holidays the agent's family received food and other gifts from the MSS officials. The agent described the gifts as "things I would not expect my best friend to give." He was told to return to the PRC at least every two years to be debriefed. If he preferred, he could be met in Hong Kong or Macao. They would pay for his travel.

During the weeklong series of lectures, the source was told that he was being groomed for use as a long-term agent and that, after completing his studies, he should consider applying for permanent residence in the United States; the MSS would assist him in this process. If he desired, a transfer to Taiwan or Hong Kong could be arranged in time. If he elected to pursue this career he would be paid and would accumulate additional compensation in the form of a retirement income, which he would receive upon returning to China.

After completing the training session the agent was offered a several-day tour of Beijing, which he declined due to time constraints. He returned home and later attended a fifth meeting (and farewell banquet) with provincial MSS personnel and a high-ranking MSS official from Beijing. The agent was given train tickets to Beijing and $2,500 in U.S. currency, for which he signed a receipt.

In analyzing the agent's description of his recruitment, several interesting facets should be noted. First, the MSS became aware of the source's intent to study abroad via the PRC government bureaucracy. The source filled out paperwork, some of which presumably went to the MSS. So apparently the MSS is structured to spot potential agents among the pool of Chinese students who travel abroad. China sends approximately 40,000 students overseas annually.[19]

Second, the MSS made use of its resources in identifying this individual and assessing his ability to conduct espionage. The recruitment process took place over six months. The time invested, as well as the ministry's foreknowledge of the source's personality and apparent prospects for academic achievement, indicates a well-planned and carefully regulated process of development and recruitment.

A third point involves the MSS's choice of themes used in "pitching the agent." These were primarily sentimental and practical. The MSS attempted to exploit the individual's emotions by appealing to his love of country and family. The prospects of good standing in the Party, plus success and high achievement in the PRC, showed the practical side of cooperation. Secondary motivational factors were the implied threats of not being permitted to travel to the West in the case of noncompliance, and government retaliation ("no future") in the case of betrayal. One can reasonably assume that references to having "no future" indicate long-term imprisonment or even execution. It is not known whether the PRC would attempt to harm individuals overseas. However, the general perception among dissidents is that the Chinese government is capable of this type of retaliation.

Case officers involved in the recruitment process were sensitive to the personal concerns and needs of the prospective agent, even though in an authoritarian environment of the PRC this might not seem necessary. The authorities rescheduled interviews and training sessions around the source's schedule. The payment received by the agent on departure was roughly equal to seven years of wages for the average Chinese worker (the per capita annual income is $370).[20]

In addition, by giving extravagant presents the handlers made it appear that they were truly concerned for source's welfare and that of his family. Taken together, the MSS case officers' actions created an impression of interestedness and personal friendship, as well as a sense of obligation on the part of the agent. Use of these techniques suggests training or experience in conducting psychological assessments and investigative interviews.

It is also noteworthy that provincial as opposed to national officers conducted the recruitment effort. It is possible that provincial MSS offices have the authority not only to recruit overseas agents, but to conduct clandestine operations that extend outside the PRC. The agent's emergency contact and clandestine communication instructions led back to his home province, supporting the contention that MSS operations can be run at the provincial level. In addition, the officers told the agent that they could meet him either in the PRC or in Hong Kong, indicating that they were the ones running the operation.

Other PRC government agencies such as embassy representatives of the state education commission and the Ministry of Public Security have tried to recruit student informants by threatening and intimidating individuals and their families. Even the MSS's attempts to recruit student informants, which occur within weeks or even days of the prospective agent's overseas travel, seems crude compared to the recruitment process used in the case of this long-term agent.[21] From the available evidence, the variance in the techniques used on PRC nationals appears to be largely dependent on the intelligence objective.

Another interesting element of this recruitment process is the degree of OPSEC enjoyed by provincial MSS case officers working in the relative safety of their own environment. Even after the source, a PRC national, was successfully recruited, trained, and paid, the MSS officers maintained their cover as representatives of the province's foreign affairs bureau. And yet the clandestine nature of their relationship with the source was always stressed. The handlers repeatedly cautioned the agent about his behavior and the risks of communicating with the PRC. They also demonstrated an awareness of U.S. communications intelligence (COMINT) efforts, if not their actual capabilities.

The MSS-provided emergency contact numbers were associated with the provincial COSTIND office. The purpose of this point of contact is not clear. However, there are two possibilities: (1) because the agent had a background in the hard sciences, the telephone number afforded some cover whenever he needed to communicate with the MSS; or (2) the MSS transferred operational control of the agent to COSTIND. Although the known relationship between the MSS and COSTIND is that of collector and customer, the agent's background makes it likely that his future clandestine collection activities would address COSTIND's information requirements. Other sources have reported that COSTIND maintains its own clandestine collection capability due to the level of technical knowledge required in the fields on which it focuses.[22]

The MSS's methods of recruiting, training, and deploying long-term agents reveal some interesting operational characteristics and capabilities. The MSS has a strategic, patient outlook when it comes to espionage and a reasonably inexpensive means of establishing illegal agent networks overseas. The requirements of writing letters approximately every three months and traveling to Hong Kong every two years, as well as the prohibition against contacting the embassy, indicate that the MSS is aware of foreign counterintelligence efforts (in this case, those of the FBI) and seeks to practice good OPSEC in order to minimize risks to case officers and agents. Recruited agents are told early in their training that their personal well-being is worth more than any piece of information.

Particularly engaging is the fact that the MSS planned to have this agent apply for immigration to the United States. This arrangement has been offered to other long-term agents as well.[23] For this to happen, a network of agents holding U.S. citizenship must be in place. One purpose of this network is to sponsor a Chinese national for U.S. citizenship. This takes at least five years once an individual is granted permanent resident status. Therefore, using the technique of recruiting agents and sending them overseas, the MSS would have to have placed long-term agents in the United States at least as early as 1986. If the MSS recruited just one percent of the fifteen thousand Chinese students who travel to the United States each year, there would be a minimum of several hundred long-term agents operating here. A survey conducted in 1991 by the Harvard Chinese Student Association on behalf of the National Coordination Committee on Chinese Student Affairs indicates that 30 percent of the six hundred Chinese students and scholars questioned plan to seek permanent residency in the United States.[24]

It is logical for the MSS to attempt to capitalize on this opportunity by recruiting agents among this population. Those students with relatives still in the PRC are particularly susceptible to MSS recruitment pressures.

The second type of espionage operative recruited is the short-term agent. Chinese students studying abroad are recruited to collect information against overseas dissidents.[25] The objective is to recruit a large number of agents at minimal cost. The account that follows is based on the recruitment of two short-term agents, Shau Huaqiang and Masami Yosshizaki.[26]

Recruitment techniques employed by the MSS show some common themes as well as some situational differences. Both prospective agents were contacted by provincial MSS officers just days before they were to leave the PRC. Shau was offered the opportunity of working for the MSS while overseas. Recruitment pressures included the promise of a good job and housing on returning to China, financial stipends while abroad, and patriotism and loyalty to the PRC. In addition, the MSS raised the prospect of not allowing Shau to travel if the recruitment offer was refused.[27]

Shanghai MSS officials arrested Yosshizaki and accused him of being a prodemocracy activist. He was told that because he was of Chinese ancestry and had a son living in China, he was a Chinese citizen, despite the fact that he held a Japanese passport, and was therefore subject to Chinese law. He was threatened with jail or execution if he refused to cooperate and was not allowed to take his son out of the PRC. If Yosshizaki cooperated, officials promised, he would be financially rewarded in six months on his return to Shanghai.[28]

Both individuals were required to sign an agreement, Yosshizaki's was more than one hundred pages long. No clandestine tradecraft training was offered to either agent; in both cases, they were told of their information requirements only in the most general terms.[29]

Short-term agents assigned to monitor dissident groups reportedly communicate information by anonymous letters to the education section of the nearest PRC embassy or consulate.[30] They also file their reports during personal meetings with consular education officials. Such meetings are held routinely on college campuses with all overseas Chinese students. Contact at the PRC embassy or consulate is kept to a minimum.

Short-term agents are also deployed against Chinese dissident groups for domestic intelligence purposes. The recruitment techniques, however, are different. The MSS and MPS routinely arrest individuals suspected of involvement in "counterrevolutionary" activities. Under physically arduous conditions, the prospective agent is offered the chance to cooperate.[31]

A recruited agent in Tibet reported that if he agreed to cooperate "they would give me all the facilities I needed, a car, a motorcycle, or a bicycle, financial support, advantages if problems occurred with other Tibetans or Chinese, a walkie-talkie to contact them."[32] Unconfirmed reports in 1989 and 1990 indicate that recruited agents were paid 400 yuan, a typical month's salary for the name of every political criminal supplied.[33]

Recruitment of agents among refugees in border areas follows the same pattern: threats and physical abuse in the case of noncooperation, financial rewards for compliance. The PRC has established intelligence centers along its border with Vietnam. According to the Vietnamese press, twenty-four such facilities existed at one time.[34]

Vietnamese and international refugee organizations have detailed PRC attempts to recruit low-level espionage agents from the flow of refugees leaving Vietnam.[35] Relocation centers in China such as the Dongxing and Fangcheng camps were fertile grounds for agent recruitment.[36] Open-source reporting indicates that border area recruitment is conducted by PRC public security officials and military personnel.[37] These entities work together closely at the district level, reflecting Mao's concept of "People's War" in its most basic form. In remote areas local inhabitants are often separated by artificial borders imposed by nations; such is the case on the PRC-Vietnam and PRC-Burma borders. As a result, local inhabitants on one side of the border are recruited to gather information from relatives or friends on the other side.

The agent recruitment process used in border areas is simplistic but can claim some successes. Vietnamese press reports in the 1980s detail a number of cases in which spies were recruited in China while living near the border or trying to flee Vietnam. Hanoi accused the PRC of using open-air border markets as a way to lure Vietnamese nationals into China, where they could be recruited.[38] Their espionage training reportedly varied, as did their information objectives.

The PRC's intelligence apparatus exhibits diversity and adaptability in its recruitment methods, which differ according to the prospective agent's individual attributes and the operational conditions at the time. The MSS is still, however, uncomfortable with recruiting Westerners as espionage agents. This is likely to change over time, however, as contact and familiarity between the two cultures increase.

Summary

The MSS is an aggressive intelligence service that is coming of age in the international arena. The combination of a rapidly developing economy and an increasingly competitive global economic environment will force China to rely more heavily on the illegal acquisition of foreign technology in its quest for modernization. The theft of advanced technology via Hong Kong has proven to be a reasonably safe, cost-effective, and productive operation for the MSS. The ministry can be expected to play an active role in supporting China's economic and military modernization by continuing to acquire technology in this manner.

The disintegration of the Soviet Union and the closure of American military bases in the Philippines is likely to create a power vacuum in Asia. Although sensitive to the concerns of the Association of South East Asian Nations (ASEAN), China can be expected to exploit this opportunity to expand its influence in the region. In addition, China is seizing a greater economic role in regional and world affairs by attempting to expand its commercial markets. The PRC increasingly makes use of arms sales to gain hard currency and develop political influence, particularly in the Middle East. China's diplomatic recognition of Israel in 1992 was also meant as a way of influencing events in that volatile region. The MSS will be required to produce intelligence to support this assertive role in the global commercial and political environments. Clandestine collection operations and covert action campaigns against foreign governments and commercial industries should therefore receive increased emphasis.

Western policy, intelligence, and law enforcement agencies must adjust the focus of their collection and counterintelligence operations if they are to contend effectively with the MSS's clandestine activities. At the policy level an increased emphasis on protecting commercial intelligence and monitoring illegal technology transfer issues is needed. In the United States, the notion of government helping private industry to protect itself from foreign intelligence activity is controversial. Providing industry with foreign high technology and economic intelligence, as practiced in the PRC, is not a policy option in the United States. For that reason, presidential administrations must supply strong leadership and thoughtful guidance to private industry on the issue of safeguarding sensitive advanced technology and corporate trade secrets.

Washington must establish the type of relationship with business that promotes the mutual development of policy guidelines for protecting sensitive technology. Such guidelines will be difficult to develop and implement due to the necessity of maintaining the domestic free flow of ideas. The legislative and judicial branches of government must also be made aware of the seriousness of illegal high-technology transfers and their potential impact on U.S. national security.

At the working level, intelligence and law enforcement agencies must redirect their operational focus and allocate the appropriate resources to specialized area studies, analyses of PRC intelligence tradecraft, and linguistic capabilities. The shifting of U.S. counterintelligence concerns is likely to be a long, slow process due to fiscal restraints, competing agency interests, and bureaucratic inertia. Congressional oversight of this process may be wise, because intelligence bureaucracies tend to be self-perpetuating and therefore resistant to change. Another impediment to effective action against Chinese espionage is the state of relations with Beijing established by the Bush administration. Privately, FBI agents say that "in the scheme of things these days, it seems to make very little difference to Washington whether the Chinese are spying or not . . . it's almost an annoyance when an actual violation of law surfaces."[39]

Given the institutional problems involved in altering the focus of U.S. counterintelligence efforts, the MSS will probably continue to penetrate and exploit the United States' and other Western nations' political, academic, industrial, and technological institutions. As the MSS expands its operations globally, its methods can be expected to increase in sophistication as well.

Part Three
China's
Intelligence
Community

Chapter 8

Military Intelligence Department

T he Military Intelligence Department (MID) of the PLA's General Staff Department (GSD) is the second largest organization in the PRC involved in HUMINT collection. Known as the Second Department (*Er Bu*), it is similar to many such organizations all over the world in that it is charged with providing timely intelligence support to the military command structure.[1]

The function of the GSD is to implement and monitor the policies of the central committee's Military Commission (MC) and to run the daily affairs of the PLA.[2] So one would expect that the GSD and MC are the primary recipients of finished intelligence produced by the Second Department. Other consumers would be the Ministry of National Defense (MND), the headquarters of the different services, the military-industrial complex, and unit commanders.

The chief of the Second Department is Maj. Gen. Xiong Guangkai. Xiong is a veteran military intelligence officer in his late fifties.[3] He is responsible to a deputy chief of the GSD, Gen. Xu Xin. Born in 1921, Xu is a native of Lingshou, Hebei. He is a veteran of the Korean War and a 1957 graduate of the Soviet Union's military academy.[4] Xiong's personal assistant is Col. Li Ning.[5] Li is considered one of the new breed of professional intelligence officers in the Second Department. He was a military attaché based in London during the late 1980s. While there, his principal intelligence activities were identifying new markets in the Middle East for Chinese arms exports and illegally acquiring advanced technology with military applications.[6]

In 1990 he completed graduate work at Johns Hopkins University's School for Advanced International Studies in Washington, D.C.[7] The Second Department's HUMINT collection activities support three types of military intelligence requirements: tactical, strategic, and technological. At present the bulk of the MID's efforts is still dedicated to the tactical intelligence task of identifying and assessing potential military threats on China's borders. This focus is likely to continue to change – in light of the diminished Russian and American military presence in Asia — as the PRC attempts to secure a more prominent position in regional affairs; collection and analysis of politico-military and military-economic information will have to increase to support Beijing's regional aspirations. The responsibilities of the Second Department can be divided into the following categories:[8]

Order of battle – The size, location, equipment, and capabilities of armed forces (military and insurgent) that exist in immediate proximity to the PRC. This should include those of the Commonwealth of Independent States, Mongolia, Afghanistan, Vietnam, Thailand, Burma, India, Cambodia, Taiwan, North Korea, South Korea, and Japan as well as American forces in East and Southeast Asia.

Military geography – The terrain features of neighboring countries.

Military doctrine – The operational philosophy, plans, and targets of currently and potentially hostile nations.

Intentions – The military intentions of current and potential enemies, their allies, and neutral nations.

Military economics – The industrial potential, agricultural capabilities, military technology level, and strategic reserves of other nations.

Biographical intelligence – Information about foreign military officials, including all aspects of their personal and professional lives.

Nuclear targeting – Facilities intelligence to support China's strategic missile forces. The size, location, and vulnerability (hard vs. soft target) of foreign political, military, intelligence, and population centers.

Military intelligence watch centers – Basic and current intelligence for immediate use and midterm planning. It defeats the purpose of military intelligence collection not to have a system in place for bringing the most recent information to the attention of policymakers and military commanders. The function of such a system is to provide indications and warnings of potential or impending military threats. It can be assumed that the Second Department maintains a network of regional and national "watch centers" to support various levels of command. The degree of autonomy possessed by military regions (MRs) – as evidenced by Deng Xiaoping's trip to Wuhan to seek the support of MR commanders during the Tiananmen crisis – means that intelligence watch centers (as well as the ability to disseminate information in a timely manner) probably exist in each military region to support that specific level of command.

The Second Department is also active in the field of high technology, especially if there are military applications.[9] In fact, according to some accounts the MID is China's preeminent intelligence agency in this regard.[10] Based on the limited number of PRC military attaches, the Second Department does not appear to have the overseas presence necessary to be the nation's primary collector of foreign high technology; but since many Second Department personnel serve under cover as consular officers, the number of collectors may actually be quite high.[11]

Due to its close relationship with the consumer – China's military-industrial complex and armed forces – the Second Department likely has some measure of authority in the planning and conduct of intelligence operations designed to acquire foreign military technology. The established lines of responsibility concerning high-technology espionage have precedent in the relationship between the KGB and the Soviet military's chief intelligence directorate, the GRU, the latter more narrowly responsible for collecting military-technological information.[12]

Chapter 9

Departmental Structure

The MID must have a structure that supports HUMINT collection operations domestically and abroad to fulfill information requirements from tactical commanders, the military-industrial complex, and military and civilian policymakers. Logically, there must be some way of compiling and prioritizing these collection requirements to accomplish tasks and to prevent duplication of efforts. For example, on a tactical level if each division commander of Guangzhou MR's two group armies and ten infantry divisions[1] wanted to know the order of battle of Vietnam's armed forces, there should be some way to centralize those requests within that MR so that the intelligence can be disseminated and the task of collection and analysis is not repeated over and over.

The focus for the collection and dissemination of intelligence supporting tactical-level requirements takes the form of a regional intelligence center. Intelligence seems to be passed to other MRs at the headquarters level. This process appears to parallel that of the PLA's civilian counter-parts, where information exchanges occur at the regional level. For example, "to strengthen the cooperative relationship among Chinese military personnel stationed in Hong Kong and Macao, the director of the Political Department and the chief of staff of the General Staff of Guangzhou Military Region cooperate in exchanging intelligence. . . ."[2]

Tactical information is collected by the PLA, PLA navy, and PLA air force reconnaissance units.[3]

PLA and PLA navy special operations units conduct visual reconnaissance and electronic intercepts for combat unit commanders.[4]

PLA reconnaissance elements exist at the company level in group armies (GAs) and MR border units. Each PLA GA is roughly equivalent to a U.S. Army corps. Border units are one part of the MR structure; the others are garrison and internal defense forces.[5]

The composition of these forces can vary among MRs due to area-specific tactical requirements. However, regardless of the composition of forces, the combat unit commander dictates the conduct of his reconnaissance unit's collection activities.[6]

Each service arm collects, compiles, analyzes, and disseminates through its own intelligence analysis center, which exists under the intelligence division headquarters in times of peace. In wartime the collection and analysis functions would be placed under the direct control of the front command.[7]

As MR combat forces are ultimately subordinate to a national command structure, so too are MR intelligence collection units subordinate to the Second Department at the national level.[8]

It is not known, however, exactly to what degree the Second Department may allocate collection duties to tactical forces. PLA doctrine encourages commanders even in the lower echelons to be aggressive and to conduct independent reconnaissance activities to meet their intelligence needs.[9]

The relationship between national and tactical military intelligence collection, analysis, and dissemination appears to be quite similar to that defined by the U.S. military's Tactical Intelligence and Related Activities (TIARA) system. Tactical commands are expected to know their own intelligence requirements intimately. While those commands forward the information they collect to national agencies, they do not respond to national-level requirements.

The contention that MR intelligence forces are coordinated at the national level is supported by the fact that the Second Department maintains a tactical reconnaissance bureau (*Jun Jiancha Zhu,* or Second Bureau) to foster communication among intelligence division commands in each MR.[10] Also at work in the MRs is the Second Department's First Bureau, which divides its collection responsibilities among five geographic divisions: the Beijing area, Shenyang, Shanghai, Guangzhou, and Nanjing. The First Bureau is one of seven functional entities within the Second Department that allows HUMINT collection and analysis work to be conducted along functional lines. These comprise two collection bureaus, four analysis bureaus, and one newly formed research bureau dedicated to science and technology.[11]

The First Bureau focuses its collection efforts primarily on Hong Kong and Taiwan. However, it also collects against targets worldwide.

The Beijing office (which is itself sometimes called a bureau) has considerable stature among the five divisions because its operatives target foreign nationals in Beijing. It also serves as the contact office for all the other divisions, meaning that these other area divisions must coordinate their activities with Beijing when they extend beyond a single area of operations. The Beijing division also assists Shenyang and is known for its use of "abnormal channels for collection." This refers to activities in the Beijing area such as the use of two hotels for collection purposes. One of those hotels is the Yellow Dragon (Huang Lung), which serves military intelligence officers training in or passing through Beijing. It also houses military intelligence personnel returning from overseas assignments. Recruitment targets are billeted in the Yellow Dragon to make the information-gathering process easier for the Beijing division's intelligence officers.

The five geographically defined divisions also conduct clandestine intelligence operations overseas. For example, the Shenyang division collects information on Russia, Eastern Europe, and Japan. These activities take place throughout China as well as in those overseas operational environments. These targets were no doubt selected based on the geographic location of Shenyang in northeastern China. Logically, North and South Korea should be targets of the Shenyang division; however, no information is available to support this assertion. One of the targets that made the Shengyang office famous is the Orient Express. Some of the workers on this train, which crosses northeastern China on its way to Russia and Europe, are either intelligence officers or recruited agents reporting to military intelligence officers in Shengyang.

The Guangzhou division also appears to collect against targets based on geographic proximity. Its primary targets are persons in Hong Kong, Macao, and Taiwan. Case officers make extensive use of commercial covers. For example, a vice president of the China Resources Holding Company (*Hwa Ren Jituan*) in Hong Kong is traditionally a military case officer from Guangzhou. This officer coordinates the collection activities of other intelligence personnel operating under Hwa Ren cover. The division maintains several other cover companies in Hong Kong and Macao as well.

The Shanghai and Nanjing divisions do not operate against nations in their immediate vicinities. Instead, they target Western Europe and the United States, respectively. Intelligence officers from these divisions are frequently required to travel in China and overseas. One reasonable explanation for this seemingly odd division of responsibilities concerns the evolution of China's military intelligence requirements. As China has opened to the West over the past two decades, its need to gather information on foreign nationals both domestically and abroad has increased accordingly. Therefore, traditional collection operations against geographic targets should have expanded to accommodate the increased number of recruitment targets. Shanghai is a major city with a number of European targets, while Nanjing hosts a number of U.S. academic exchange programs (see Chapter 6).

At the national level the Second Department's HUMINT program includes PRC military attaches who collect in support of strategic military intelligence requirements. These individuals belong to the department's attache bureau, which contains more than four hundred people. The attache bureau, also called the Third Bureau, is subdivided into several groups (*Xiao zhu*) on the basis of geography as well as the significance of that area to attache collection operations. One of the most important of these groups, and also presumably one of the most active, is based in Turkey. Another group is based in Africa. The operational centers of other groups are unknown.

PRC military attaches collect data on foreign weapons technology, order of battle, and military doctrine, economics, and policy. While much of this information is available from open sources, sensitive technology generally must still be approached in a clandestine manner. These attaches fulfill their responsibilities by conducting both overt and clandestine HUMINT operations. In their circles this sort of work is called "half open."

Because PRC military attaches have clandestine collection responsibilities, an internal training program is needed to develop these skills. Espionage tradecraft would be covered, as would foreign languages. The requirement to compartmentalize information and the secretive nature of intelligence organizations dictate that this course of study should be offered by a separate entity under the Second Department, rather than by the training academies of other military departments or civilian agencies. The Nanjing Foreign Affairs Institute – recently renamed the PLA Institute for International Relations – is the Second Department's school for espionage tradecraft and foreign languages. In addition, the Third Department has its own educational facility.

The Second Department has its own analysis bureau to process and disseminate military intelligence. Personnel from this bureau conduct preliminary all-source intelligence analysis. The term all-source refers to the use of information from all intelligence disciplines – human-source intelligence (HUMINT), signals intelligence (SIGINT), and imagery intelligence (IMINT) – in reaching analytical conclusions. Each day at 7:00 a.m., the analysis bureau produces a report of the significant military intelligence events that occurred over the previous twenty-four hours. The report is circulated to members of the central committee's Central Military Commission (CMC), the politburo, and chiefs of the general departments. The bureau is located in building no. 11 of the GSD's Beijing headquarters. Due to the presence of SIGINT and IMINT, access is restricted to a greater degree than it is at other bureaus.

The analysis bureau works with the China Institute for International Strategic Studies (CIISS) (*Jungguo Guo Zhanlue Yanjiusuo*), also known as the Beijing International Strategic Studies Association (*Beijing Guoji Zhanlue Xuehui*). Established in 1979, the institute defines itself as "an academic body for research on international strategic problems established to study strategic questions in relation to national security and world peace and to develop academic exchange with strategic research establishments, organizations, and academics abroad."[12]

The CIISS does not openly identify itself as an element of the GSD or the Second Department. However, almost all of the institute's employees are former or current PLA officers. In the case of the latter, personnel often divide their time between the institute and the Second Department.[13] Beijing's reasons for not publicly associating any of its so-called research institutes, civilian or military, with intelligence agencies are unknown. In the case of the CIISS, one reason may be the desire to avoid tainting the institute or limiting its contacts with foreign specialists in relation to strategic and national security problems. In his book *The Making of Foreign Policy in China: Structure and Process*, sinologist A. Doak Barnett notes that "perhaps [the CIISS's] main function at present is to develop contacts with specialists on strategic and national security problems abroad." Within the Second Department the CIISS is called "our window on the world."[14] Given the Chinese habit of using academic institutions for intelligence purposes (see Chapter 6), such contacts would logically be exploited as channels for recruitment and collection.

Other well-known PRC academic institutes also conduct research and analyses on military doctrine, strategy, and tactics, although their relationship to the military intelligence community is unclear. The Academy of Military Science (AMS) and the recently created Society of Military Science (SMS) are "engaged in the study of military science under the leadership of the CMC."[15] Regardless of their formal relationship to the PLA command structure, both these organizations appear to have influence with PRC military policymakers. Personnel in both institutions comprise former and current military officers – frequently those who have overseas experience as military attaches.[16] Given the subject matter of the research and its importance to military policy planners, it is likely that some form of ongoing information exchange occurs among the AMS, SMS, and CIISS.

The AMS is considered to be the center of the PLA's military science studies as well as an advisory group and think tank for the CMC and general departments.[17] Its Foreign Military Affairs Research Department (FMARD) is dedicated to studying international military issues. In 1990 it contained the following subdepartments: the United States; Western Europe; the Soviet Union and Eastern Europe; and Japan and Asia-Pacific.[18] The FMARD offers guidance to the CMC, general departments, PLA units, academies, and research organizations on matters under its purview.[19]

The SMS was founded at the All-Army Work Conference on the Study of Military Sciences held in Beijing on 10-12 January 1991. The objectives of the SMS include sponsoring research activities in military science, appraising the results of such activities, and promoting foreign exchange programs in the field.[20]

The Second Department has three intelligence analysis bureaus in addition to its analysis unit (which conducts preliminary analyses only) and its associated military research institutes. The first two of these three bureaus produce and disseminate in-depth intelligence analyses about specific geographic targets. One of these offices – known as the Fourth Bureau – concentrates on the political and military policies of the Commonwealth of Independent States and Eastern Europe, while the other, the Sixth Bureau, focuses its efforts on the Asian nations that border China.[21]

The other component of this trio is called the America/Western Nations Analysis Bureau or the Fifth Bureau. It uses primarily open-source publications in its political and economic analyses. Analysts on the American side of this unit tend to stay there for many years, because this particular specialty appears to carry prestige in Chinese intelligence circles. Also, it probably takes considerable time and effort to develop a language-capable intelligence analyst who can recognize the cultural and political nuances reflected in American and European open-source publications. The Fifth Bureau's two favorite American sources are congressional reports and papers produced by the RAND Corporation.[22]

Institutions (academic or otherwise) that conduct research on foreign military doctrine, strategy, or capabilities are adequate only for basic or estimative analysis. The most important part of military intelligence analysis is the production of current intelligence. Just as intelligence centers in each MR support the headquarters elements of tactical commands, the CMC and general departments need to have a focal point for indications-and-warnings (I and W) intelligence in the event of a national military emergency. This military intelligence center would be required to synthesize all-source intelligence from the MRs and overseas diplomatic posts to provide timely support to national-level commands. It is likely that this center exists as a part of the analysis bureau due to that entity's access to all-source data, which would be used to confirm and detail impending military threats.

The last of the Second Department's so-called functional bureaus is the newly established Bureau of Science and Technology (also called the Seventh Bureau). This unit's role is to research, design, and develop technology. Under its management are six research institutes: the Number 58 Institute, which develops espionage equipment; the Seagull Electrical Equipment Factory, which produces technical support equipment; the Beijing Electronic Factory; the Number 57 Institute; the Northern Transportation University's computer center; and the bureau's own computer center.[23]

The very existence of the Seventh Bureau indicates that the Second Department is thinking about and planning for espionage directed against foreign science and technology well into the future. This is also made apparent by the presence of two electronics factories under the bureau's control. A well-established relationship between military technology collectors and scientific research centers is strong evidence of a clearly defined role for technical intelligence support in the development of weapon systems. Long-term planning such as this provides some insight into the quality and foresight of the management structure. Also, the Second Department clearly does not depend on its civilian counterpart, the MSS, for technical support.

A matter of great interest is the apparent emphasis on computer applications in espionage, as demonstrated by the two computer research institutes. These institutes may signal the Second Department's intention of expanding into the potentially lucrative field of computer espionage, which is ideally suited to the PRC. University and research institute computer networks can be exploited to collect classified as well as unclassified data on a range of technical subjects.

In addition to the functional bureaus involved in collection and analysis, the Second Department has a number of administrative and support bureaus and divisions. These entities are collectively referred to as nonfunctional bureaus:

Records/Archives Bureau – This unit receives and stores open-source publications from overseas. One section is called library services. One subelement of this bureau is the Foreign Military Publishing Company, which translates and republishes other nations' military journals.[24]

Confidential Bureau (*Jiyao zhu*) – Also known as the Secret Documents Bureau, this unit is responsible for handling, transmitting, and storing classified documents. In addition, it sets uniform standards for the classification levels of documents.[25]

General Management (*Zhunghe zhu*) – This unit provides Second Department personnel with logistical support in the form of transportation (cars and buses), office supplies, recreation centers, and food service.[26]

Commission Security Bureau (*Zhungwei jingwei ju*) – This unit may in fact be a division rather than a bureau. It is responsible for the physical security of CMC members and general department heads. It also has some jurisdiction in the security operations of Second Department facilities. It is reportedly one of the more powerful entities in terms of its budget and its freedom of action.[27]

Based on the number of bureaus, the Second Department appears to rival the MSS in size (see fig. 5). Another nonfunctional element within the Second Department monitors and supports the military intelligence apparatus. This is the political department.[28] This unit reports to the General Political Department (GPD) and reflects a system of Party control that is an inextricable part of the Second Department's structure. The GPD is in charge of counterintelligence as it relates to the political control and ideological education of the armed forces.[29]

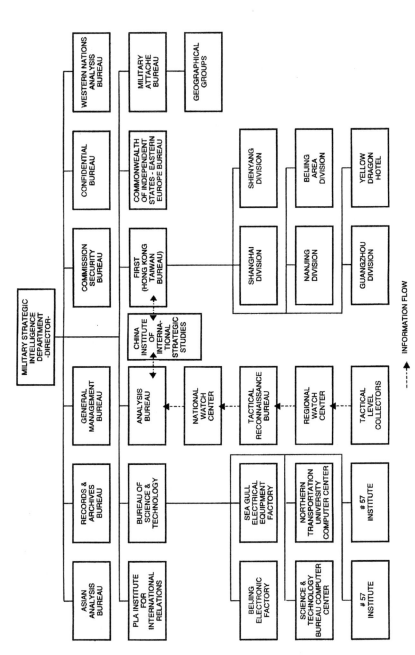

5. Military Strategic Intelligence Department (Second Department)

It is also responsible for officer appointments, promotions, and transfers of personnel.[30]

The GPD maintains two distinct and separate hierarchies that parallel the military chain of command in the form of political commissars and political committees.[31] Political departments (*Zhengzhi bu*) are the administrative arms of the political committees and are pervasive at all levels of the armed forces, much the same way that the Party's discipline inspection commissions exist in PRC civilian agencies.[32] Political departments are divided into functional subdepartments at the regimental level and above.[33]

The organizational structure of political departments varies among the PLA air force, the PLA navy, and the PLA proper. These differences are minimal and reflect specific service requirements. For example, the Air Force Newspaper Office (*Kongjun Baoshi*) is staffed by the GPD.[34] While no equivalent office exists in the PLA, the political department's propaganda department publishes the *Liberation Army Daily*. The GPD maintains propaganda departments in all three services.[35] The other major subdepartments common to all services are as follows:

General Office – Manages the work flow under the director and deputy directors. It has four subunits: the secretariat division, the administrative division, the letters of inquiry division, and the political research office.[36]

Organization Department – Responsible for the daily management of Party affairs.[37]

Cadre/Personnel Department – Handles promotions, assignments, and personnel transfers. This is one of the more powerful elements of the political department's control structure.[38]

Propaganda Department – In charge of propaganda, ideology, mass mobilization, and publications.[39]

Security Department – Oversees all security matters, including counterintelligence investigations and operations within the armed forces, physical security, and VIP security.[40]

Liaison Department – Studies the PRC's relations with Taiwan. It was formerly called the enemy affairs department. It also wages

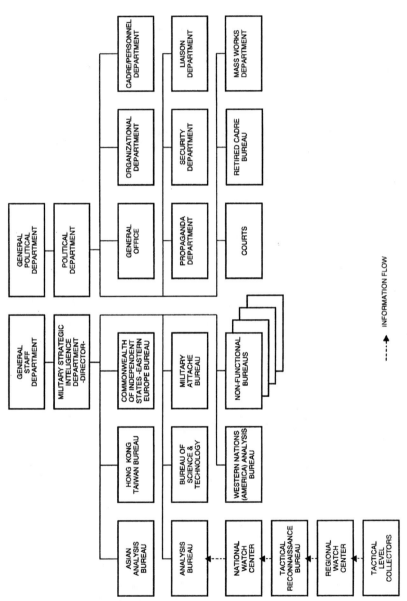

6. Military intelligence and security structure

political warfare against foreign military forces, produces positive intelligence by interrogating and exploiting enemy personnel, and conducts overseas clandestine intelligence collection operations against Taiwanese military personnel.[41]

Mass Works Department – Seeks to promote harmony among the military, the local populace, and local governments.[42]

Retired Cadre Bureau – Addresses the concerns of retired officers, including employment and housing.[43]

Courts – Works closely with the discipline inspection commission and the PLA procuratorate to try those accused of crimes.[44]

The influence of the GPD on the operations of the GSD's Second Department is particularly interesting because of the political control methods employed by the former. The political department's security departments (baowei bu) co-opt individuals within the armed forces.[45] Knowing that the GPD engages in this practice, one would expect that Second Department personnel are the primary recruitment targets for the *baowei bu*. The GPD feels that this is necessary because compartmentalization, operational secrecy, and a cadre of well-trained clandestine intelligence officers could easily present a threat to the Party's control of the military. In addition, the defection of a Second Department intelligence officer to a foreign country could easily expose a number of covert agents and damage clandestine intelligence operations.

Another role of the GPD involves conducting overt counterintelligence investigations. These inquiries are handled by the GPD's countersabotage department and fall under the broader term political cases, which refers to any act that threatens or questions the CPC's control of the armed forces. From 1986 to 1990 the PLA military court and procuratorate processed more than six hundred political cases involving low-level officers. Of these, thirty-five cases – involving more than four hundred personnel – were identified as "plots to organize counterrevolutionary cliques."[46] In effect, the GPD conducts at least part of the normal counterintelligence duties of the PRC's military intelligence service. Once the GPD is included (see Fig. 6), this intelligence apparatus appears to be quite large indeed.

Chapter 10

Military Intelligence Operations

Tactical Operations

In the PLA, specially trained units support infantry battalions by conducting visual reconnaissance. The PLA aggressively promotes the use of reconnaissance troops for collection purposes:

> Every commander must organize reconnaissance within his unit's zone of activities. He must not wait for instructions from his superior, nor must he seek his superior's decision as to whether he should organize reconnaissance. The reconnaissance he organizes must be carried out without cessation to comply with the combat mission through each successive period and phase of combat. Each new mission requires immediate organization of reconnaissance. The conduct of continuous reconnaissance during combat is vitally important.

The PLA's extensive use of reconnaissance troops and recruited espionage agents in support of military campaigns is well documented. The success of the 1962 offensive against India is partially attributable to good information collection on the part of the PLA. Indian intelligence assessments identified PLA collection activities in the North East Frontier Agency up to two years before the military offensive. The PLA gathered facts on India's order of battle, terrain features, and military strategy through agents planted among road gangs, porters, and muleteers working in the PRC-India border region. These agents later guided PLA forces across the area during offensive operations. India later discovered that Chinese agents had infiltrated commercial establishments near the border, and junior PLA commanders – disguised as Tibetans – had reconnoitered their future area of operations.[2] In addition, prior to the offensive PLA forces captured Indian patrols and inter-rogated the soldiers for order of battle information.[3] All told, the PLA had foreknowledge of the Indian army's forces, weapons, and combat tactics.

Historically, PLA tactical intelligence collection efforts have also been quite aggressive along the PRC-Laos and PRC-Vietnam borders. From the late 1970s to the late 1980s Vietnamese authorities regular-ly accused the PLA of conducting armed reconnaissance forays and dispatching recruited agents into that country to collect information – and to incite rebellion.[4]

In more specific terms, PLA border intelligence activities involve using squads, platoons, and occasionally even companies of recon-naissance forces to locate and identify Vietnam's defensive positions, troop movements, and order of battle. PLA incursions reportedly have included acts of sabotage: destroying facilities, planting mines, car-rying out assassinations, and killing farm animals.[5] These operations have occasionally resulted in skirmishes with Vietnamese public secu-rity forces. The effective range of reconnaissance troops employed in this role is approximately five miles.[6]

In addition to conducting visual reconnaissance the PLA recruits Vietnamese nationals as espionage agents.[7] Vietnamese press reports attribute these low-level agent operations to the local "secret police or intelligence organ" and reconnaissance units of the PLA. Recruitment targets often belong to one of the twenty-four ethnic minorities that account for approximately one million people living on both sides of the PRC-Vietnam border.[8] Many of these ethnic groups, and even indi-vidual families, are separated by that artificial boundary. Chinese inhabitants of southern Guizhou and Yunnan are pressured into cross-ing the border to contact relatives or to encourage Vietnamese kin to visit.[9] To assist in this process PRC authorities unilaterally opened bor-der markets to Vietnamese border-crossers.[10] The border markets reportedly stock a number of commodities unavailable in Vietnam.

The PLA's border agent operations are designed to be simple and of short duration. A number of espionage cases publicly prosecuted by Hanoi have detailed the PLA's recruiting and handling techniques. As discussed above (see Chapter 7), border agents are recruited via monetary incentives or physical torture, or both. In almost all cases the most advanced forms of tradecraft used were forged travel docu-ments, dead letter drops, and code names.[11]

The PLA Navy has also played a part in HUMINT collection

along the border. Chinese fishermen working in Vietnamese territorial waters are routinely debriefed for their knowledge of Vietnam's shipping activities, maritime economy, and coastal defense system. In addition, Vietnamese fishing vessels (probably caught in Chinese waters) have been detained and their crew members interrogated for military information. According to the Vietnamese press, attempts are made to recruit the crews of the captive ships.[12]

The PLA Navy also has tactical reconnaissance capabilities in the form of seaborne special forces called amphibious reconnaissance units (*zhongdui*).[13] These units perform standard naval commando missions: underwater demolitions, raids, and removal of underwater obstacles. Their collection activities include observations of water depths, currents, the slope of the seabed, and enemy defensive positions.[14] It is not known to what degree these forces are used in peacetime. It is interesting to note, however, that the PRC government's description of a recent amphibious reconnaissance unit exercise mentioned using dead drops to communicate with indigenous forces and kidnapping and interrogating enemy military personnel.[15] The Vietnamese and Taiwanese governments have often accused China of conducting just such activities.[16]

Tactical intelligence collection is not limited to combat reconnaissance on the PRC border. Throughout the 1980s the PRC military intelligence apparatus aggressively gathered information about Taiwan:

> The intelligence department and the combat department of the General Staff Headquarters successively sent eight cadres at and above division level to Taiwan to conduct on-the-spot reconnaissance; they made a detour through Japan and the United States to gain entry as tourists. On the basis of reconnaissance results, a "Newly Revised Combat Program for the Liberation of Taiwan" was recently completed.[17]

Another intelligence duty conducted by tactical units is covert action. Loudspeakers strung along the PRC-Vietnam border broadcast propaganda to Vietnamese troops.[18] Chinese border markets are used as distribution points for propaganda literature targeted specifically to Vietnam's national minorities.[19] Disinformation of this sort is also distributed in southern and central Vietnam by recruited agents.[20]

Although conducted and put out by tactical-level units, political-military propaganda against foreign forces is a national function under the purview of the GPD's liaison department. Implementation of a specific theme of disinformation must somehow advance national policy objectives. It is therefore probable that the GPD formulates propaganda in accordance with CMC military and policy decisions. Such campaigns are then implemented through the PLA's overt and intelligence channels under the supervision of political commissars.

Strategic Operations

Unlike tactical operations, PLA strategic HUMINT collection operations attempt to satisfy the information needs of a broad range of strategic-level forces and military-industrial consumers. These national intelligence operations are limited to supporting military and related clients. As a result, the scope of their clandestine and covert efforts is narrower than that of the MSS. The Second Department draws on national-level assets to conduct four types of strategic intelligence operations: collecting information on foreign military forces, acquiring technology with military applications, identifying foreign markets for Chinese arms exports, and conducting covert action campaigns.[21]

One of the primary tools Beijing uses to collect national-level military information is the military attaché.[22] As described earlier (see Chapter 2), a standard role of military attachés worldwide is to be an "open collector." Several recent espionage cases indicate that PRC military attaches have clandestine collection responsibilities as well. Examples include the already-discussed arrests of Second Department officers Hou Desheng, a military attache in Washington, D.C., and Zhang Weichu, working under the cover of consular officer at the PRC consulate in Chicago.[23] Both were caught trying to purchase what they believed to be classified NSA material.[24]

The significance of this attempted espionage lies in the sensitivity of SIGINT material. When communications codes and frequencies are known to an adversarial intelligence service, that service will probably attempt to intercept and decode communications signals. In the case of military communications, data collected from intercepts can include unit size, activity, and location; personnel and command structure; and radio call signs. The case of convicted spy John Walker, who sold Navy communications codes to the Soviet Union, serves as a warning of how serious this type of espionage can be.[25] As a result of

Walker's willingness to sell U.S. secrets, the Soviets were "able to decipher millions of Navy messages which would have been decisive" had a naval conflict occurred.[26]

Analysis of the Hou/Zhang case points to a lack of OPSEC in the planning and conduct of the intended clandestine operation. Hou Desheng and Zhang Weichu exposed their identities (whether in fact or by virtue of their activities) to someone they believed was a recruited agent. As a result of this error, both case officers were identified by the FBI. In addition, the two met their ostensible agent in a Chinese restaurant, indicating that no form of clandestine communication between agent and handler was employed. The fact that the FBI was able to penetrate the conspiracy and arrest both Chinese case officers means that there had to be FBI agents present in the immediate area of the restaurant, site of the arrests. Had either of the Second Department officers or a third individual monitored the area beforehand (an example of countersurveillance), the FBI presence probably would have been noticed and the operation aborted.

Hou and Zhang were almost certainly collecting in pursuance of GSD Third Department information objectives, because SIGINT operations are the responsibility of that department.[27] In 1983-84 Hou was a third secretary in his government's permanent mission to the United Nations in New York.[28] In this position, he was not acknowledged as a military officer. Yet within a year he was a military attaché in Washington. Presumably, his espionage career did not start when he was assigned to the PRC embassy in Washington, D.C. He was most likely engaged in clandestine intelligence activities while at the U.N.

Other publicly exposed cases support the thesis that the Second Department assigns case officers to conduct espionage under cover of the U.N. In at least one instance the department attempted to get hold of advanced weaponry and technology with military applications. In October 1987 Chi Shangyao and Charles Chang were arrested in Newark, New Jersey, for conspiring to illegally export to the PRC ten tube-launched, optically tracked, wire-guided (TOW II) missiles, Sidewinder missiles, and blueprints for the U.S. Navy's F-14 fighter. Chi and Chang were residents of New York City and naturalized U.S. citizens. Also named in the conspiracy were three U.N.-based PRC military officers: air force attaché Fan Lianfeng, chief military attaché Maj. Gen. Zhang Naicheng, and science and technology counselor Fang Xiaofan.[29]

Contact between the PRC's U.N. mission and Charles Chang was established by Chi Shangyao.[30] Chi was a resident of Taiwan for thirty years before coming to the United States. Chi and Chang met with Fan on several occasions; they discussed the price of the missiles ($250,000) and the need to falsify end-user certificates and shipping documents.[31] The plan was to ship the stolen items from Seattle, Washington, to the PRC via Hong Kong. According to testimony by U.S. customs agent Frank Ventura, Chi stated that he expected to be asked by PRC officials to sell Chinese-made Silkworm missiles to Middle Eastern countries if the current operation was successful.[32]

Analysis of this case illustrates the operational methodology employed by Second Department personnel and PLA information objectives.

PLA Air Force attaché Fan Lianfeng ran the operation while Zhang Naicheng monitored its progress; as minister-counselor for science and technology, Fang Xiaofan was probably responsible for confirming the technical characteristics of the pending purchases.[33] While U.S. law enforcement authorities named all three individuals as unindicted coconspirators, only Fan Lianfeng could be charged with conducting overt acts in furtherance of the crime. As a result, he left the United States immediately after U.S. customs agents arrested Charles Chang and Chi Shangyao.[34] Zhang Naicheng went on to be the defense attaché at the PRC embassy in Washington from 1988 to 1990.[35] He returned to that post in 1992.[36]

Like the case of Hou and Zhang, the Fan Lianfeng operation reveals poor use of OPSEC measures. U.S. customs agents were able to infiltrate Fan's group and record conversations. This indicates that clandestine communications methods were not used by either recruited agents or case officers. Agents were introduced to three intelligence officers rather than just the one running the operation, thus placing them all at risk. As a result the recruited agents – Chi and Chang – as well as the U.S. Customs Service investigator assigned to the case were able to identify three PRC intelligence operatives, their respective positions, and their information objectives (material acquisitions).

The most striking OPSEC failure evident in the Fan Lianfeng operation is the amount of information made available to recruited agents. Chi's statement about expecting to sell Silkworm missiles to the Middle East on behalf of the PRC, if true, identifies a Second Department methodology of using recruited agents in third countries to conduct arms transfers. This operational tactic would be similar to the MSS practice of using foreign companies to acquire desired technology (see chapter 5). Chi's statement also implies that Beijing intends to conduct such sales. Iran is one known to have received Chinese Silkworm missiles. In addition, the exposure of PLA information objectives – TOW II and Sidewinder missiles, F-14 blueprints – identifies PLA intelligence gaps, military intentions, and areas for projected armament development.

Fan Lianfeng's choice of weaponry and technology clearly indicates the Second Department's level of responsiveness to PLA military requirements. The TOW II is the United States' most technologically advanced antitank weapon for use by an individual soldier. If the PRC managed to acquire, reverse-engineer, produce, and deploy this weapon, it would significantly upgrade the nation's border defenses. In the mid-1980s, when the espionage attempt occurred, the PRC faced twelve qualitatively superior Soviet armor divisions on its northern border (the Far East strategic direction and Mongolia).[37] In addition to bolstering its military capabilities, indigenous production of a TOW II copy would have offered Beijing an added commodity for raising hard currency via international arms sales.

Much like the TOW II, the acquisition of the short-range air-to-air Sidewinder missile would have increased PLA capabilities in the areas of air combat and air defense. Without addressing the technical aspects of Sidewinder capabilities, suffice it to say that indigenous production of a Sidewinder copy would have added a significant punch to some of the PLA air force's estimated six thousand aircraft.[38] Also, technical analysis of the missile would reveal its operating characteristics and capabilities, which would ideally (from the PLA's perspective) lead to the development of countermeasures.

The acquisition of F-14 blueprints would also have helped the PLA by revealing the aircraft's operating characteristics so that defenses could be developed. The F-14 is designed to take off and land on aircraft carriers. The PLA navy could be expected to pursue this type of technology if Beijing acts on its often-debated desire to build or buy a carrier. The dissolution of the Soviet Union makes the latter option somewhat more likely as new republics try to sell naval assets in exchange for hard currency. In the early 1990s press reports indicated that the PRC was attempting to purchase the *Varyag,* a Russian 67,500-ton Admiral Kuznetsov-class carrier. The carrier was designed to carry up to eighteen Su-27 or twenty-five MiG aircraft. China has already acquired twenty-four Su-27 aircraft from Russia.[39]

A primary intelligence role of Second Department officers is to collect information or technology with military applications. But equally important is identifying foreign markets for PRC arms sales.[40] In recent years Beijing has sold advanced weapon systems or technology with military applications to Argentina, Brazil, India, Iran, Iraq, North Korea, Pakistan, Saudi Arabia, South Africa, Syria, and other countries. In several cases the technology has been used to develop nuclear capabilities.[41]

To identify foreign weapons markets for PRC exploitation, Second Department case officers recruit arms dealers. Once recruited, these dealers are used to hide the involvement of the PRC government in the illegal transfer of weapon systems – either to China via third countries, or to third countries as end consumers.[42]

The process for identifying and approaching these potential agents is interesting because of its cautious nature. The dealer's background is researched carefully before an actual recruitment pitch is made. By far the preferred choice is a dealer who has long-standing contacts with the PRC. Second Department case officers always try to avoid approaching unknown entities.[43] This policy demonstrates the attaché bureau's realization of its operational capabilities and limitations. Identifying and recruiting someone with a long-standing connection to the PRC is infinitely easier and safer than targeting a comparative stranger.

The cautious approach used in recruiting arms dealers stands in stark contrast to the actual running of the operation. The frequent press reports in the United States about people arrested while trying to ship weapon system components on behalf of the PRC are a testament to the overall poor OPSEC employed by Second Department intelligence officers. This is likely due to a lack of positive intelligence in the PRC on the capabilities and methods of U.S. law enforcement agencies. In fact, the department's clandestine operations would be far more effective if its personnel had even a perfunctory knowledge of the legal limits of physical surveillance, wiretaps, and arrests in the United States.

Public exposure of Chinese involvement in espionage, missile sales, and nuclear proliferation has provoked negative responses from U.S. lawmakers and other Western governments. By early 1991, the issue of PRC arms transfers nearly jeopardized Sino-American relations. In June of that year the United States levied sanctions on Beijing for transferring missile technology to Pakistan. Only then did Chinese policymakers publicly respond to U.S. pressure to stem the outward flow of military hardware and technology. In November, the PRC agreed to abide by the Nuclear Nonproliferation Treaty (NNT) and the Missile Technology Control Regime (MTCR). China signed the NNT on 9 March 1992.[44] In August 1993, the United States again placed restrictions on the sale of advanced technology with military applications to China. These sanctions were put in place because China continued to violate the MTCR by selling M-9 and M-11 missile technology to Pakistan. The PRC can be expected to circumvent these restrictions via foreign suppliers and covert means.

Despite Beijing's professed adherence to international guidelines on missile and nuclear proliferation, the mission of Second Department intelligence officers has not changed. PRC military intelligence case officers are more cautious than ever, but they are still active in identifying foreign markets for military exports.[45] Instead of selling completed weapon systems, the PRC provides dual-use technology, missile-related materials, and Chinese scientists to support foreign missile programs while still following MTCR guidelines. The PRC's actions appear to be motivated by purely mercantile considerations: the 1985-88 sale of CSS II missiles to Saudi Arabia netted Beijing an estimated $3.5 billion dollars.[46] Increased political influence with the recipient nation is an added benefit.

In addition to collecting information and selling military technology, the Second Department has a long history of trying to exert influence in foreign countries through covert action. In the case of the PLA, such efforts have taken the form of financial and logistical support to insurgents. In addition, the PLA has trained personnel from a number of organizations in guerrilla tactics.

In the early 1960s, guerrilla warfare schools for foreigners were established at the Nanjing and Wuhan military academies. Throughout the decade PLA officers trained insurgent groups from Algeria, Angola, Botswana, the Cameroons, the two Congos, Guinea, Indonesia, Kenya, Malawi, Malaysia, Mozambique, Niger, Nigeria, Portuguese Guinea, Rhodesia, Rwanda, South Africa, Thailand, and a number of other third world countries.[47] PLA personnel were very active in subverting postcolonial governments that recognized nationalist China on Taiwan or were in some other way opposed to Beijing's revolutionary ideology. Military and intelligence training programs were conducted by PLA intelligence officers in China, Southeast Asia, and Africa.

The role of PRC intelligence personnel in military covert action operations deserves further attention. PLA experts on weapons and combat tactics are the logical choice as teachers of foreign insurgents. The role of intelligence personnel in military assistance programs is generally limited to managing and financing the effort, arranging for covert logistics, and developing agents (unilateral penetrations) within the group being trained. The following chronology outlines some of the PLA's covert activities:

1960
– A guerrilla warfare school for foreigners is established in Beijing. Recruits are from Colombia, Cuba, Ecuador, and Peru.

1964
– A total of 225 African insurgent groups are trained in guerrilla warfare in PRC military academies.

– In Nepal, a Chinese technical expert defects and identifies a Chinese road-building project as a front to subvert the Nepalese government. Five hundred PLA soldiers are operating under civilian guise to funnel arms to pro-PRC agents. PRC military attaché Col. Kan Mai is declared a persona non grata.

– In Brazzaville, French Congo, Kan Mai assumes his new position as first secretary in the PRC embassy. He also manages two training camps for Congolese rebels at Gamboma and Impfondo.

– In the Sudan the PRC embassy is implicated as a supplier of arms and money in the unrest that led to the overthrow of the government.

– In Bujumbura, Burundi, assistant cultural attaché Tung Chipeng defects and reveals the Chinese embassy's support of a revolt in the neighboring Democratic Republic of the Congo. Diplomatic relations are severed, and the PRC mission is expelled.

– In Burma the PLA supplies the "White Flag" communist insurgency while officially supporting Rangoon's nonaligned government.

1965
– Kenya expels NCNA journalist Wang Teming (known to hold the rank of major in the PLA) for directing the attempt to seize the headquarters of the ruling Kenyan African National Union. Also, the Chinese embassy is denounced and an employee is expelled over illegal weapons shipments.

– In Tanzania, the Chinese embassy is implicated in a plot to overthrow the government of neighboring Malawi.

– In Singapore Chinese intelligence officer Sim Siew Lim is arrested along with twenty others for plotting to assassinate government leaders.

– The Thai Patriotic Front is established in Beijing.

– In Indonesia a coup attempt by the pro-PRC Indonesian Communist Party (PKI) is brutally suppressed. The PKI is financed by China.

1966

– In the Central African Republic a cache of weapons and ammunition bearing "foreign markings" is discovered. That country severs relations with the PRC; the embassy staff, NCNA personnel, and thirty Chinese nationals are expelled.

– The Chinese mission to Dahomey is expelled for running operations against Upper Volta (now Burkina Faso), Togo, Niger, and Nigeria.

– The ruler of Ghana, Kwame Nkrumah, is overthrown while on a visit to China. Relations with the PRC are severed and 430 Chinese military and intelligence personnel expelled.

– The Malayan National Liberation League opens a mission in Beijing.[48]

1973

– In Zambia and Tanzania PLA military personnel under the guise of railway engineers direct military operations by insurgents against the Rhodesian government. Two military training camps are established: one in Zambia near the Tate province of Mozambique, and one in Tanzania.[49]

1975

– The Front for the Liberation of Angola (FNLA) is trained, armed, and supported by the PRC. China sends 119 PLA instructors to an FNLA base in Zaire.[50]

1980-88

– In Afghanistan PLA military personnel train and equip the Mujaheddin resistance. Training centers are located in Pakistan and China's Xinjiang province.[51]

The Second Department's most recent large-scale covert effort was the arming and training of the Afghan resistance. This operation is significant because it identifies what must be considered current (or at least recent) intelligence doctrine and methodology in the support of PLA covert activities. In addition, the fact that it was undertaken at all clearly indicated Beijing's feelings about the Soviet presence in Afghanistan and its willingness to take limited military steps in the face of a world power.

The PLA supported antigovernment rebels in Afghanistan during nearly the entire course of the Soviet military presence.[52] That support consisted of organizing, financing, training, and arming resistance groups. Afghan government officials and Western media sources allege that the PRC's covert military activities were financed by the CIA.[53] Whether or not this was the case, it makes sense to assume that some communication occurred between the United States and China over military support for Afghan resistance groups, if only to reduce duplication of effort.

The PLA began offering small arms and financial support to Afghan resistance groups in 1980. By February of that year at least six groups were competing for Chinese and Pakistani funds. From 1980 to 1984 the cost of PRC support totaled approximately $400 million.[54] Captured Chinese-made weapons were regularly put on display at press conferences in Kabul; these included assault rifles, heavy machine guns, mortars, and recoilless rifles.[55]

By September 1984 the PRC was supplying artillery pieces (107 mm and 122 mm) to the rebel forces.[56] The 107-mm Type 63-1 (the "63" refers to its year of production) appears to be the PLA's standard twelve-tube rocket launcher; it has lightweight alloy tubes and weighs approximately 300 pounds. It is not clear whether China provided the 122-mm Type 60 high-velocity copy of the Soviet D-74 howitzer gun, or the older Type 54 copy.[57]

In 1986 the PRC increased its support and started to supply 130-mm antiaircraft guns to rebel groups. The Type 59-1 field gun is similar in design to the Soviet M-46, but with a range of only 22 km instead of 27-31 km. Chinese support continued to escalate throughout the 1980s, eventually including 12.7-mm Type 54 heavy machine guns, to be used on single antiaircraft mounts; 14.5-mm Type 58 Soviet ZPU twin antiaircraft heavy machine guns; and 37-mm Type 55 towed antiaircraft guns, which are obsolete but are exported to several countries.[58]

The PLA provided these weapons to a number of resistance groups it helped to establish: "Victory," "Guards," "Immortal Flame," and "Paikar."[59] Presumably some of these organizations operated as part of the openly Maoist National United Front of Afghanistan.[60]

The PLA maintained a large military training presence along with supplying weapons to Afghan rebels. Until 1985 the PLA had approximately three hundred military advisers at training facilities in Pakistan. The camps were located in the following areas: Muhammad Gard, 2 km south of Nawagai; Shabqadar, 20 km northwest of Charsadda; Lwara Mena, 12 km northeast of Landi Kotal; and Faqir Abad, near Peshawar.[61] In February 1985 the PRC opened additional training camps on its own territory near the population centers of Kaxgar and Hotan in the Xinjiang Autonomous Region.[62] The PLA instructed Afghan rebels in the use of Chinese weapons, explosives, and combat tactics as well as the applications of propaganda techniques and espionage tradecraft.[63]

Presumably the PRC did not train the Mujaheddin training in espionage tradecraft just for the rebels' sake. It is quite likely that the PRC exploited the resistance members by effecting unilateral penetrations. As a matter of standard practice the Second Department would attempt to recruit some of the guerrillas it trains to serve as clandestine collection agents. Ideally, a number of these persons would assume positions in the new government if their resistance movement were to succeed. Afghan government officials believe that the resistance movement was exploited by the PRC for espionage purposes and that the MSS was also involved in collection operations.[64]

Chapter 11

Secondary Intelligence Organizations

Anumber of civilian agencies and military departments in the PRC have HUMINT collection or analysis responsibilities. These agencies have limited information objectives and resources, compared to the MSS and the GSD's Second Department. Also, there is a management structure that oversees the activities of the Chinese intelligence community on behalf of the CPC.

Insight into the identities, operations, and goals of these organizations offers a more accurate picture of China's overall HUMINT collection capabilities. In addition, even general knowledge about the size and information objectives of these agencies gives us a more balanced view of PRC intentions regarding the future conduct of clandestine HUMINT operations.

General Political Department, Liaison Department

The GPD has intelligence collection responsibilities in addition to its role in co-opting PLA military personnel. Its Liaison Department (*lianlu bu*) is openly responsible for studying relations with Taiwan, coordinating propaganda, and interrogating POWs.[1] However, this department conducts clandestine intelligence operations as well. The Liaison Department deploys case officers overseas under commercial covers to collect information on Taiwan.[2] Presumably, the primary targets of this unit are Taiwanese military personnel.

The department's case officers are known to be deployed in Hong Kong, Singapore, and the United States. The illegal covers used in these countries are generally storefront operations or executive positions in overseas Chinese companies.[3] The Liaison Department apparently does not place its intelligence officers under official diplomatic cover. It is likely that the overseas presence of this unit is minimal, given the limited scope of its information objectives.

Liaison Department case officers are reportedly well-educated and experienced midlevel officers.[4] Their paths for disseminating information to the various PRC intelligence services are linear ñ that is, channels are restricted within each agency.[5] Consequently its reports are not collated with those of the Second Department.

Commission of Science, Technology, and Industry for National Defense (COSTIND)

This agency has both overt and clandestine collection capabilities and functions.[6] It has offices at the provincial level and in the fourteen ministries involved in military production. COSTIND is in charge of research and planning for military technologies and weapon systems. It makes recommendations concerning military technology and weapons acquisition to the administrative office (bangongting) of the Central Military Commission. These recommendations are often coordinated with the Academy of Military Sciences, the National Defense University, the GPD, the GSD's Equipment and Technology Department, and to some extent the Ministry of Foreign Affairs.[7]

COSTIND assigns research projects to ministries with military production responsibilities. Those ministries in turn pass the work to the research institutes under their auspices, and the institutes send their information and technology requirements back to COSTIND. The commission relies primarily on the Second Department but also on the MSS to acquire — illegally — the needed foreign technology. In addition, due to the high level of technical knowledge necessary, COSTIND personnel engage in espionage by attempting to steal foreign technology with military applications, primarily from the United States.[8]

The commission sends its scientists overseas as members of academic and scholarly exchanges to collect information and to identify needed foreign technology or weapon systems. Once the material is identified, acquiring it becomes the job of either the MSS, the Second Department, or COSTIND, depending on the availability of resources and access.[9] The very nature of this collection practice lends itself to tremendous duplication of effort.

COSTIND personnel routinely travel to the United States and Western Europe as employees of the New Era Corporation (Xinshidai) to buy and arrange for the delivery of technologies not cleared for export. The New Era Corporation, established in 1986, and Poly Technologies (*Baoli*) are in fact agencies of the Chinese military that oversee weapons imports and exports. Another ostensibly independent firm used in arms transfers is the Xingxing Company, part of the General Logistics Department.[10]

New Era is a direct subordinate of COSTIND. For the purpose of dealing with foreigners, Poly Technologies was established as part of the Chinese International Trust and Investment Corporation (CITIC). However, in reality it remains under the GSD, which makes all decisions on operations and personnel. The Equipment and Technology Department has jurisdiction over the company. The current president of Poly Technologies, Col. He Ping, is married to Deng Xiaoping's daughter, Deng Rong.[11]

It is not clear whether other companies are also used to obtain foreign technology illegally; however, New Era and Poly Technologies have ties to the China North Industries Corporation, the China Precision Machinery Import-Export Corporation, the China State Shipbuilding Corporation, the Great Wall Corporation, the China Electronic Import-Export Corporation, the China Aviation Technology Import-Export Corporation, and the China Nuclear Energy Industrial Corporation (see fig.7).

On one occasion in the mid-1980s New Era employees traveled to Boston and illegally purchased and transported shipboard navigational equipment not cleared for export. As a standard security measure, only the Chinese ambassador to the United States and the second secretary in charge of intelligence activities received advance notice of the secret operation. This type of collection activity appears to be representative of COSTIND's method of operation. Specific technologies of interest are identified in foreign companies. COSTIND personnel, under cover as employees of New Era or Poly Technologies, travel to the company to purchase the desired item. It is transported to the nearest PRC facility—in the 1986 case, this was the Chinese embassy in Washington, D.C.—where it is shipped via diplomatic pouch to Beijing.[12] The same method of operation has been used by PRC military-industrial corporations since 1979, which predates the creation of COSTIND.[13]

Another method used to acquire technological information is to invite foreign experts to China. Under the guise of academic institutions, COSTIND invites noted scientists and academics to lecture at

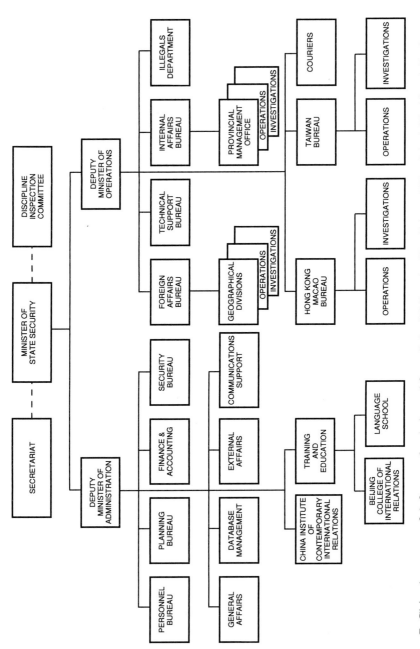

7. China's system of defense sales (adapted from John W. Lewis, Hua Di, and Xue Litai, ìBeijingís Defense Establishment: Solving the Arms-Export Enigma,î International Security 15 [Spring 1991]: 89)

Chinese universities. This method of exploiting visiting scholars is a time-honored practice of the MSS and the Second Department (see chapter 6). Generally, COSTIND covers all expenses for visiting scientists and their families. After the scheduled classroom lectures, "special sessions" are held for the commission's experts.[14]

It is likely that some of the experts who attend foreign visitors' special sessions are from COSTIND's Intelligence Research Institute. Unlike the agency's technical research centers, this institute conducts research and analyses on such broad issues as the application and management of science and technology in military industrial development. Specifically, the institute supports the macromanagement and decision-making bodies of science, technology, and industry for national defense. In addition, institute analysis supports strategies for weapon systems development and structural reform in the defense technology sector. The Intelligence Research Institute edits and publishes a journal, *Guofang Keji Yaowen* (Important news about science and technology for national defense), that runs articles on military technology and trends in armament development.[15]

Chinese Communist Party, Investigations Department

The CPC's Investigations Department was all but eliminated in the reallocation of resources that took place when the MSS was established in 1983. The department does maintain a small staff to conduct political investigations on behalf of the Party's central committee.[16] For example, Investigations Department personnel were part of the security teams deployed to Chinese embassies to investigate the activities of student dissidents in the wake of the Tiananmen Square protests.[17] Based on the available evidence, it appears that activities directed specifically at the Party are considered political in nature and justify the involvement of the Investigations Department. These kinds of activities are viewed somewhat differently than those of hostile foreign intelligence activities, which are seen as directed against the government and society as a whole.

New China News Agency (NCNA)

The New China News Agency (Xinhua) traces its roots to 1931, when it was founded as the Red China News Agency. It adopted its current name in 1937 and is China's primary news service abroad and at home.[18] The NCNA deploys hundreds of journalists overseas to collect foreign news, which is disseminated in China and abroad. NCNA publications in the PRC carry a variety of classifications that limit their distribution.

The most well known of the NCNA's domestic publications is Reference News (*Cankao-Xiaoxi*), a daily compendium of foreign news articles translated into Chinese. It is an internal (*neibu*) publication, meaning that it is distributed only to Chinese citizens. Approximately nine million Chinese have subscriptions to Reference News. The reason that distribution is limited to PRC nationals is that the foreign articles are intentionally mistranslated or otherwise altered to support the Party's authoritarian control.[19] Reference News thus serves the dual purpose of giving the populace a view of the outside world and giving the Party a way to manipulate Chinese public opinion.

A somewhat more restricted neibu publication is Reference Material (*Cankao Ziliao*), a collection of translated news articles on significant international events and foreign views of the PRC. The bulletin is available in morning and afternoon editions, each of which is nearly one hundred pages long. Based on the number of articles translated and sent daily to Beijing, it is likely that Xinhua's overseas journalists spend a significant amount of their time supplying material for Reference Material. The publication appears to be available only to higher-ranking cadres (as of 1984, those at or above grade 13). Some analysis of foreign news articles is included. Abridged articles are noted as such.[20]

Another classified bulletin produced by the NCNA is Internal Reference (*Neibu Cankao*), covering events in the PRC as reported by PRC sources. Internal politics is a sensitive topic for the CPC leadership; as a result, this journal's distribution is even more restricted.[21] NCNA's Internal Reference is circulated to officials at the level of deputy minister and above. Each ministry also publishes its own internal reference sheet specific to its area of responsibility.[22] A small sampling of these publications follows:

Selected Edition of Documents on Wages and Welfare —Collected and edited by the Ministry for Metallurgical Industry. Classified: internal

Encyclopedia of Business Management — Edited by the compiling committee of the Taiwan Harvard Business Management Book Series. Classified: internal

Monthly Bulletin on Results of Scientific and Technological Research — Published by the Science and Technology Documents Publishing House, Beijing. Classified: internal
Electronic Market — Published by the Fourth Machinery Industry Ministry. Classified: domestic
Foreign Trade Survey — Published by the Research Institute for International Trade, Ministry of Foreign Trade. Classified: internal
Finance Research — Published by the Finance Research Institute, Ministry of Finance. Classified: domestic
Foreign Reports Reference — Compiled by the foreign news editing department of the NCNA. Classified: internal
Foreign Language Press Materials — Published by the NCNA. Classified: internal
Domestic Philosophical Trends, Internal Reference of World *Economy and Politics, Economic Research Reference Material, Foreign Literature Trends, and Soviet and East Europe Problems* — Published by the Chinese Academy of Social Sciences. Classified: internal[23]

Chinese Communist Party, United Front Work Department

The CPC's United Front Work Department (*Tongzhan Gongzuo Bu*) has a long history dating back to the formation of the Party. The department has covert action and clandestine collection duties.[24] Its acknowledged responsibility is to carry out PRC foreign policy with nongovernmental (noncommunist) organizations.[25] In this sense it may be said to conduct covert action by attempting to influence organizations in other countries in support of Chinese foreign policy objectives ñ for example, manipulating overseas Chinese organizations into lobbying their government on a particular issue. On a more mundane level, the task of persuading Chinese scientists overseas to return to the PRC belongs to the United Front Work Department.

In addition, the department conducts clandestine intelligence operations. Its case officers work under cover of the Second Foreign Affairs Bureau, in the Ministry of Foreign Affairs, and their recruitment targets are limited to Chinese nationals with connections to Taiwan. It appears that the department serves as the civilian counterpart to the GPD Liaison Department. A noticeable difference is that the former operates under diplomatic or legal cover. As of the late 1980s two United Front case officers worked out of the PRC embassy in Washington, D.C.[26]

Political Legal Leading Committee (PLLC)

Formerly known as the Political and Legal Affairs Commission, this body is an element of the CPC. Press reports indicate that it is responsible for the overall management of China's intelligence community.[27] However, that management role is limited.

The newly appointed head of the PLLC is Ren Jianxin, the former president of the supreme court, who replaced the well-known Qiao Shi.[28] Qiao was born as Jiang Zhitong in 1924 on the island of Dinghai, Zhejiang province. He attended the East China Associated University and has served as deputy head of the CPC's United Front Work Department and head of the International Liaison Department. He is a member of the politburo, the standing committee, and the CPC central committee and secretary of the Party's Central Committee for Discipline Inspection.[29] Qiao is generally well respected as a professional intelligence officer who has stayed above the fray of CPC political infighting.[30]

The PLLC manages not only intelligence agencies but also the law enforcement and judicial structure.[31] It is under the direct control of the CPC Military Commission, and its most important function is to maintain internal order. The following agencies are known to be under the direction of the PLLC: the MSS, the MPS, the People's Armed Police, the Discipline Inspection Committee, the procuracy, and the judiciary.[32]

The PLLC's role as a supervisory body over the PRC intelligence community is limited to collection and analysis functions as they relate to internal affairs.[33] There appears to be little supervision of foreign intelligence activities at the policy level ñ and only with the approval of the CPC Military Commission secretariat. PLLC offices at the district, province, and county levels supervise internal operations by serving as the central point for of communication between local intelligence and law enforcement agencies.[34]

Part Four
Conclusion

Chapter 12

Future Prospects

Throughout this work I have tried to present an accurate picture of the structure, operations, and methodologies of China's intelligence services. It should be noted, however, that there is a tendency among people to view foreign intelligence activities in terms of spies with superhuman attributes engaging in daily life-and-death struggles. One could therefore interpret this work as some kind of call to arms to prevent waves of Chinese spies from subverting the Western world. It is not.

Like much of the PRC government, China's intelligence services just do not work – or at least not very well. Virtually anyone (surely any foreign scholar) who has come into contact with the Chinese bureaucracy can attest to its many limitations. In terms of efficiency the system is inefficient and often hopelessly bogged down in its own red tape. The omnipresence of the Party, so necessary for internal control, is an impediment to the effective administration of government at all levels. The new positions announced for senior party members at the Fourteenth Conference in October 1992 are a clear indication that the Party seeks to integrate itself further into government entities. A good example of this process is the appointment of Qiao Shi as chairman of the standing committee of the National People's Congress on top of his party positions.

As a reflection of the Chinese communist system, PRC intelligence operations in Western nations are characteristically poorly conceived and executed. This is not to say that PRC intelligence services have not succeeded in exploiting friendly relations with Western nations and secretly extracting information from private and government institutions. In fact, they have been quite successful in this regard, and in conducting covert operations by manipulating foreign governments through paramilitary training efforts, arms sales, technology transfers, and disinformation campaigns. It is, however, not the quality but the sheer numbers of these operations that enable a portion of them to succeed. The number of clandestine intelligence operations conducted by the PRC overwhelms Western counterintelligence and law enforcement agencies. In addition, the PRC's limited information objectives, focused on midlevel technology, puts much of its intelligence activity below Western governments' threshold of concern.

Another way to view PRC-sponsored espionage is in the context of worldwide intelligence activities. More than likely, all major powers conduct espionage to support their interests. In this setting, China is no different from other nations with global interests. Also, gathering information on friends and adversaries should not necessarily be viewed as an evil act. Often, lack of knowledge about another country's intentions serves to destabilize relations between states. Particularly in the military arena, in many situations foreknowledge of a nation's intentions can lead to diplomatic or other policy initiatives that can avert a costly arms race or even military conflict.

Simply put, espionage is a normal activity between nations. It is extremely rare for the conduct of espionage to affect bilateral relations between states. However, one cannot accept the premise that the PRC is simply executing a government function by engaging in espionage. Beijing's strategic intelligence objectives include suppressing political opposition and developing its military-industrial base and force projection capabilities. The latter objective tends to be an especially destabilizing factor in the region.

The significance of China's strategic intelligence objectives can be seen in geopolitical and military terms. In essence, concern about China's clandestine intelligence activities centers on the premise that there is a fundamental difference between protecting one's national security through espionage and using it as a military or economic force multiplier. With this difference in mind, Chinese intelligence operations come to seem significant in proportion to a country's prospects for economic competition or military confrontation with the PRC. Also, China's intelligence support for its nuclear and missile proliferation activities alters regional balances of power and is therefore of concern to nations with a stake in world order.

Any country that determines that China's (or any other nation's) espionage activities present a threat to its interests is likely to respond with security, law enforcement, and intelligence actions. To be effective, these responses draw on detailed knowledge of the adversary's structure, objectives, and procedures. In this respect, Western intelligence services are handicapped in their ability to analyze China's clandestine intelligence operations. The logical result is an inability to neutralize those efforts.

The handicap of Western intelligence services stems from a limited base of knowledge about China's language, government, and culture. Naturally, this lack of knowledge hampers our ability to understand everything from the PRC's decision-making process for international arms sales to its application of resources to suppress overseas Chinese dissidents. Of course this shortcoming does not exist universally or to the same degree in all Western intelligence and law enforcement agencies. However, in the United States the number of people who speak, read, and write Chinese is truly minuscule. This number becomes smaller when one restricts the field of consideration to government service, and smaller still when it is narrowed to the law enforcement and intelligence communities.

One example of behavior peculiar to Chinese society (and government) is the use of personal contacts or guanxi networks in daily life. Personal contacts are a reasonably universal means of conducting business, in the intelligence field as elsewhere. However, in China these guanxi networks have evolved into a highly developed mode of overcoming bureaucratic obstacles such as internal compartmentalization, interagency turf battles, poorly defined criminal codes, and government administrative regulations. Personal contacts are based on family connections, geographic origins, friends, and school classmates.

Another peculiarity of the Chinese government and its intelligence services is their inability to keep most information secret. The existence of this book is evidence of that tendency. Information tends to flow freely in China because close family and other personal relations frequently serve as conduits. In China, these "leaks" are explained by the adage, "little road, little news" (*xiaodao xiaolu*). Much of the information I received in the course of research was reported in a characteristically Chinese fashion – everyone seemed to know someone who knew someone who heard that. . . . As a result, even the most closely guarded government secrets can be heard on the streets of Beijing. The analyst's task then becomes separating fact from fiction.

In the U.S. intelligence community second- and third-hand information is jokingly called rumors intelligence (RUMINT). Analysis of this material requires in-depth knowledge of the culture and unfettered access to multiple sources of reports for comparative analysis. For the latter task, proficiency in the Chinese language is a must. Western intelligence and law enforcement agencies generally have few of these assets.

For Western nations to analyze the actions of PRC intelligence organizations, traditional concepts of HUMINT operational methodology will have to change. As described throughout this study, the operational methodology of the Chinese intelligence apparatus is unique. For example, the Chinese blur traditional Western definitions of intelligence officer (case officer) and recruited agent (spy). As a result, PRC intelligence officers risk exposure by actively stealing information and technology themselves, instead of recruiting a target-country national for that purpose.

Another unique characteristic of Chinese operational practices is the extensive use of commercial, academic, and other illegal covers. The use of such covers by civilian and military intelligence agencies appears to rival in number their use of legal diplomatic covers. This approach to espionage tradecraft is inherently more risky. As discussed in chapter 5, the number of Chinese citizens arrested in Western countries (primarily the United States) for conducting illegal technology transfers on behalf of the PRC government points to the frequent use of illegal covers by Chinese intelligence agencies, and the fact that relatively few Westerners are caught indicates that this technique is used less frequently.

From the available evidence, two conclusions may be drawn concerning the future of the PRC's intelligence apparatus. First, Chinese intelligence services will become more sophisticated and will be unaffected by Western intelligence and security practices. Increased contact with the West, combined with long-term planning by the MSS and the Second Department, will likely increase the effectiveness of operations in support of China's foreign policy, its military-industrial sector, and ultimately its force projection capabilities. Second, due to the recent expressions of political dissent, the government can be expected to maintain or even magnify its emphasis on elements of control in Chinese society. With the expansion that is already in progress and the prospect of more on the horizon, China's intelligence services will soon come of age in the international arena.

Appendix 1.
Translation

A Summary of the Meeting of Educational Counsellors (Consuls) in Chinese Embassies and Consulates

Note:

In March, 1990, the State Education Commission convened a meeting of educational counsellors (consuls) in Chinese embassies and consulates and the speakers included He Dongchang, vice chairman of the State Education Commission, Teng Teng (on the situation in the Soviet Union and Eastern Europe and a propaganda program prepared by the Party's Ministry of Propaganda), officials from the Ministry of Public Security and the Ministry of National Security (on policies concerning the Front for Democracy in China, the Chinese Alliance of Democracy, and other organizations), Zuo Zhengfeng from the Foreign Ministry (on policies concerning the United States and Canada), officials from the Party's Ministry of Organization (on Party organizations among the Chinese students and scholars in the United States and Canada). He Dongchang summed up the main points presented at the meeting and an abstract of the meeting was signed by Li Peng. The content of the meeting, which closely concerns the Chinese students and scholars in the United States and Canada, is broken down into several subjects that are introduced as follows.

1. International and Domestic Situations

—The basic theory of Marx's scientific socialism is not wrong; the idea that Marxism-Leninism is out of date must be firmly criticized.
—The changes in the Soviet Union and Eastern Europe did not

represent the mainstream of history; they were serious setbacks in the development of socialism.

— The failure of Ceaucescu lay in disassociation from the masses, poor management of economy and the Soviet intervention.

—The present international situation is similar to that of the 1894-1914 period, when capitalism made some headway in a peaceful environment and the international labor movement was disrupted by the opportunism that emerged from the Second International.

—The New Thinking of Gorbachev is a more thorough negation of Stalin and is not doing any good to the international communist movement.

—The changes in the Soviet Union and Eastern Europe have brought about difficulties. The hard time for the peoples of these countries has just begun. Economic reform cannot be accomplished in an unstable situation. Eastern Europe's foreign debts total 170 billion [sic] and the current foreign loans are just enough to pay the interest. Poland's open market is economically unsound. The Soviet Union faces the problem of Lithuania. Now each West German state covers an East German district, Bavaria covers Hungary and Czech. East Germany is an exception. Other Eastern European countries are going to have a hard time.

—The Soviet Union is confronted with critical social and nationality crises. The economy has deteriorated and many anticommunist organizations appeared.

— China persists in its reform, which is not social democratism, but a self-improvement of socialism.

— The strong point of our Party is that it has not been influenced by social democratism. The ten-year reform has been fruitful, otherwise we would not have been able to resist this worldwide upheaval.

— Institutions of higher education constituted the area that was hit most by the disaster. Only one third carried on routine work. A considerable proportion of grassroots organizations lacked strength and was involved in the riot. In few universities, the riot was endorsed by the authorities, such as Shenzhen University, whose president has been removed from his post by Guangdong province.

— After the incident of Romania, counter-revolutionary slogans have increased. The changes in the Soviet Union, apparently quiet, also had some influence.

— During the winter vacation, college students conducted surveys. The people were basically content, especially about the consumer prices and the anti-pornography campaign. However, there was still discontent about the Party's corruption.

— The problems involving the Party's corruption should be exposed, but it is not allowed to negate the leadership of the Party in the name of anti-corruption.

— In the past ten years, news media failed to provide proper guidance for public opinion.

* The negation of Mao Zedong thought means the negation of the history of the Chinese Communist Party. The Soviet Union negated Stalin thoroughly.

— Last year we won a great political victory; economy and the ideological front have also taken a better turn, and yet we cannot expect an immediate improvement of the situation, which will take a long time.

— In the domestic market, the price of food has dropped while that of clothing has risen. Industry is facing difficulties; consumption and mass purchase have been curbed. In Jiangxi province, the cost of dinners and banquets at the public expense has dropped by 80 percent. At present, the market is slack, large quantities of products piling up. For instance, the No. 1 Auto Factory has 30,000 vehicles to be sold. Nevertheless, last year's agricultural output was better than the year before.

— 3.5% percent of the workforce has been laid off at the national level and some of them will have to go back to rural areas. Electric machinery is the sector suffering the greatest difficulties.

2. Policy Concerning the Chinese Students and Scholars in the United States and Canada and Instruction to Embassies and Consulates.

— The work on exchange students and scholars should be given a higher regard and be perceived as an international struggle and an anti-brain-drain fight. We should hold the banner of patriotism high and at the same time, expose and strike at a small group of people. This is a long struggle. Our diplomats are carrying out an arduous task fighting in the front. Now it is a struggle of life and death. Every embassy, every individual has to rely on its or his/her own and, consequently, it is allowed in many cases to take action without first asking for instructions.

— The United States holds the exchange students and scholars as hostages, so we should not push them. Our embassy people must view this problem from the standpoint of a struggle and should not limit their work to routine management of student affairs.

— It is impossible to bring all the exchange students back. We should be realistic. Our policy is to expand progressive force, win over the middle-roaders, and isolate the reactionary. Our struggle should be based on righteousness, benefit, and constraint. In a way, the Party work is underground. Party organizations in the U.S. cannot openly conduct their activities.

— There are exchange students who love the motherland, but they do not like socialism very much. We should look at this correctly and work hard. We should also see that the situation is improving in China.

— We must expand the first category, protect them and support them, even if they only make up a few percent. We must correctly treat those who have wavered and distinguish them from those who are against the government. The people we rely on can be divided into two types, those who have been always steadfast and those who have wavered once.

— Our policy must be exemplified with the second, the third, and part of the fourth categories. We can set up a few good examples in regard to passports.

— The strikes aimed at our opposition must be well calculated. There is no hurry to deal blows to those who are still hidden. The strikes should be divided into different stages and our first targets are those who are disliked even by upright Americans.

— The lesson to be drawn in the case of the United States is that the Party's work failed to follow up promptly. Those who are firm should be organized, those who are not so firm can be kept in touch, whereas those who are reactionary should be done away with. Our goal is to make most patriotic and some return. It will be worth the effort, even if we can get a few percent who still hold socialist ideas.

— We must try hard to win over the masses in the middle and our slogans and aims must be appropriate. Do not say that the majority of exchange students have no feelings for the motherland. They only want to stay a little longer and save up more money, which weakness was explored by the Independent Federation of Chinese Students and Scholars (IFCSS). We must inspire the students with patriotism.

— Student work should give priority to development of Party organizations and control of Friendship Association of Chinese Students and Scholars. We must oppose the activities of IFCSS, FDC (Federation for Democracy in China) and CAD (Chinese Alliance for Democracy).

— We have to speak in two different tones. Publicly, we talk about patriotism and lawfulness. To Party members and other backbone members we should also talk about socialism and communism. Some backbone members should be placed in the third echelon that remains under cover. They must be ready to replace those in the second echelon.

— We should form some intermediary organizations, such as clubs devoted to recreation activities. They should not sing a high tune; instead, they should try to win over those middle-of-the-roaders who are inclined to side with us.

— It must be said in public open statements that the government has no intention of abandoning the students and withdrawing the demand that they return to serve the motherland. It is understandable that they are not returning in the immediate future for various reasons. If they think they need more time, we can extend their stay. We can also help those who have difficulties. We believe that the majority are patriotic; we will be happy to see them return; however, if they choose to stay, we will not press them to come back. Then we can extend passports for a few students. It will certainly have a favorable influence.

— Some have changed their J-1 visas into F-1 visas and these can be treated as self-supported students. However, distinctions must be made; some can be allowed to renew passports. We welcome them to pay back the training fee; if they do not pay, we will not force them. We can neglect such trivialities. In that case they owe us our kindness, but it must be made clear what is right and what is wrong. No matter whether they pay it or not, they are at fault. For a small group of people (about 10%). their passports should be handled on an individual basis. As for the reactionary backbone members, their exchange student status, Party membership, job status back at home should all be suspended. They should not be allowed to come back to China. The majority still love the motherland and this love will prey on them in the long run. Their life in the West is not easy.

— As for those who have been naturalized, so long as they correct their mistakes with action (to return to China), we will not hold them responsible for it.

— We will temporarily suspend state-sponsored exchange student programs with the United States and Canada and only send visiting scholars. For those who hold job positions, if their work units do not agree to let them go to visit their spouses abroad, they can be allowed to resign. Do not call it expulsion. If 5 percent exchange students come back, it will be even better than 100 percent, because these have been tempered in the fire.

— Efforts must be made to ensure the return of the students in the first category. We have to keep in touch with the academic front. Those who return should be properly assigned. From now on, we will not send these young people out. A total of 7,000 have gone from 36 institutions. As a result, the work has been affected.

— It is not right to send the students abroad before they work at home and gain some knowledge of the situation in China. This has made it difficult to recruit graduate students at home. Because of the "five-year" provision, many do not want to pursue graduate studies. They only want to use the domestic graduate programs as a springboard to enable them to go abroad, so it is better to terminate such programs. It must be made clear that students must work at home first before they go abroad or that they are only allowed to receive training at home.

— We have failed in sending abroad students of social sciences. However, we should tell exchange students that if they can combine what they learn with things in China, love the motherland and socialism, what they learn will still be useful.

— The problem of IFCSS is complicated and should be studied carefully. If we declare that it is a counter-revolutionary organization, how shall we deal with the majority of students? We are going to withhold this declaration, but we must deal blows to those ringleaders. We cannot allow them to hold the reins.

— On January 7th, the Ministry of Public Security declared that the passports of Wan Runnan, Chen Yizhi, and Yan Jiaqi have been voided. There are over one hundred ringleaders in FDC, CAD, and IFCSS. We have contacted the Foreign Ministry and the Ministry of Public Security to void their passports at different stages, mainly: 1) the top leaders who take as their goal to overthrow socialism and subvert the government, such as the core figures of FDC, CAD and the Democratic Party; 2) those who have instigated the riot, and conspire, organize, attend or provide materials for the U.S. Congressional hearings; 3) those who publicly seek political asylum; 4) leaders of the newspapers and radio stations that persist in opposing the government and the Party and openly carry anti-Party messages; 5) those who collude with anti-China, anticommunist forces both at home and abroad and work hard to seek donations. The first blow can be dealt to five or six people in the first category. We should single out those whose reputation has been compromised, such as Wu'er Kaixi.

— In dealing with IFCSS lobbying activities, we should say that it is understandable that the majority got involved in order to stay, but the ringleaders, such as Liu Yongchuan and Han Lianchao, should be dealt with harshly.

— To strike the ringleaders, we should give them a bad name. During the anti-Japanese war, we used the name "han jian" (traitors to China). Now we must think of a name that has a resounding effect; we cannot use the word "dissidents".

— After we adjust our policies to the reality, we must unite more students around us so as to prevent the United States from repeating this trick. The current policy is made on the basis of the composition of different forces among the students. What we try to accomplish is to win over the middle-of-the-roaders, strike at one extreme, and consolidate the other.

3. Party Organizations among the Exchange Students

— Organize those Party members who have stood firm to conduct regular Party activities, three to five to a group. In cases where necessary conditions are not met, keep in touch on a person-to-person basis. Those who are not clear in their minds should be kept in touch with designated members and watched; if there are no positive signs, they can be left alone for some time.

— As for those members who have obtained permanent residence permits (mainly in Canada), as long as they still love the motherland, their membership shall not be suspended and they can be regarded as special members. The membership of those who have accepted Western ideas and openly opposed the Party should be suspended.

— Those who violated the Party principles and encouraged others to withdraw from the Party should be kicked out. Membership abroad should be handled according to concrete circumstances. Those who are willing to withdraw from the Party may be allowed to do so after it has been confirmed. Those who renounced their membership because of confusion or threat but later on requested to nullify their renouncement should be dealt with on an individual basis, such as taking some disciplinary measures or being put under observation. Those whose signatures were put on the declaration of renouncement without their own knowledge should not be counted as having renounced their membership.

— Strengthen Party organization. Kick out some or allow them to withdraw some, and keep those who have been behaving well. The latter may also be kept in touch on a person-to-person basis. Party members must receive training before going abroad and their organizational relations should be handed over to the embassies and consulates.

— A document issued in 1981 provided that if a member has lived an extended period abroad, his or her membership should be suspended and put in another category during the Party census. If a state sponsored student or scholar has not kept in touch with us or failed to pay membership fees for one year, he or she should be regarded as having voluntarily given up their membership.

— Party organizations exist to carry out struggles, in which they can keep vitality. Only when Party organizational work is well done can we successfully manage the students. In the United States and Canada, Party organizations have collapsed and there are no longer Party activities, but Party members are still there. Those who joined the Party with the intention to change it cannot be regarded as Party members.

— The first thing on our agenda is to control Party organizations; the second is to control Friendship Association of Chinese Students and Scholars. Our demands should not be too high or pressing. We can work like underground organizations, find a few reliable ones in each school and form a Party branch. The backbone members can stay abroad.

4. Sino-American and Sino-Canadian Relations

— In his talk about the resumption of the Fulbright Exchange Program with China, Oksenburg said that the Americans did not wish to stir up riots among the Chinese students either.

— At present, the Sino-American relations has plunged almost to the bottom since the low ebb after the "June, 4th event". The U.S.

government did not respond strongly to the lifting of martial law and the release of political prisoners, although it expressed some signs of general welcome. The Report on Human Rights brought about new strains on the bilateral relations. We cannot expect that the relationships will improve in the near future.

— The prior consensus of the two U.S. parties on Chinese policies has split into two oppositions. One side thinks that China has lost its vital position in the big triangle or at least the position has been largely weakened. At present, the reforms are declining. Modernization needs capital and technologies, for which China largely depends on the U.S. Therefore, economic sanctions can force the Chinese government to give in. The other side maintains that the stick and the carrot should be used in combination. Although China's position in the triangle declines, its strategic position, which restrains Moscow and exerts influence on West Asia still cannot be neglected. Therefore, it is necessary to maintain dialogues while denouncing the "June 4th event" so as to pull China back on the track of reform. This is also the viewpoint of the Bush administration. But the bottom line is that the "June 4th event" should not be disregarded.

— Bush's basic approach is: 1) maintain the status quo; 2) keep the pressure; and 3) leave some latitude. The two sides share the same intention and the difference lies in the assessment of the situation. We may make use of the difference between the two sides. Bush presses on the issue of the overseas students, and appeases on the issue of the satellite.

— The resolution to the issue of overseas students relies largely on the internal factors, but also on the external factors to a certain degree. We should provide an adequate explanation for the outside world and exert pressure on both the U.S. and Canadian governments. We protest the executive order of the Bush administration and further contact with the U.S. government will depend on our needs.

— Bush has two cards in hand: the Report on Human Rights and the report on the "five-year provision"; the Congressional discussion of the most favored nation status next May. The U.S. government regards the issue of the overseas students as a big bomb on us.

— We do not have many cards in hand. They are the Fulbright Exchange Program, continuation of exchange students, the UN peace maintenance forces and release of the political prisoners. We do not release our response hastily so that the U.S. government will be kept in the dark. Our success in exposing and striking the ringleaders of IFCSS will add pressure on both the U.S. and Canadian governments.

— The "five-year provision" concerning the self-supporting students was only announced among ourselves, which was a blow to the U.S. government. We should stick to it. The newspaper *"Hua-Sheng Bao"* released the entire document. We do not care much about this release.

— The Sino-American relations will not improve very much unless the U.S. sanctions are removed. The policies concerning the exchange students will not change, either.

— The pressure on the Canadian immigration policies should be maintained. Teng Teng and Liu Hua-qiou are in charge of contacting the Canadian government on this issue. We temporarily suspend sending students to Canada. However, this is not long-term policy. The difference between the U.S. and Canada is that the U.S. expects the students to go back to help with the modernization, but Canada allows immigration so as to brain-drain China. We need to sign an agreement on this issue with the Canadian government in the near future.

— The pressure on China will further increase if the U.S. has its way with the Soviet Union.

使领馆教育参赞（领事）会议精神

说明：

国家教委于三月份召开了使领馆教育参赞（领事）会议，会上讲话的有国家教委副主任何东昌，睢膝（苏联，东欧形势及中宣部宣传提纲），公安部，安全部负责人（对民阵，民联等组织的政策），外交部左政铎（对美，加政府政策），中组部负责人（美，加留学人员中的党组织工作）。会议由何东昌作总结，并由李鹏批发会议纪要。会议讲话内容与美，加留学人员有密切关系，现分几个方面介绍如下。

一．国际国内形势

○ 马克思的科学社会主义基本理论没有错。要坚决批判马列主义过时论。

○ 苏联，东欧形势的变化不代表历史发展的主流，是社会主义发展进程中的严重挫折。

○ 齐奥塞斯库的失败在于不联系群众，经济搞不好，还有苏联插手。

○ 目前国际局势与1894--1914年相似，资本主义在和平时期得到发展，国际工人运动出现了第二国际机会主义。

○ 戈巴乔夫的新思维比赫鲁晓夫更恶毒否定斯大林，对国际共运没有好处。

○ 苏联，东欧的变化带来了困难。他们人民的苦日子刚刚开始。动荡下搞不好经济改革。东欧外债有1788亿，现在外裸刚够还利息。波兰采取开放市场政策，在经济上是行不通的。苏联还有立陶宛的问题。西德目前一个州包东德一个区，巴伐利亚包匈牙利和捷克，东德是倒外，其他东欧国家日子欲不好过了。

○ 苏联存在尖锐的社会民族危机，经济下降，成立了许多反共组织。

○ 中国坚持走改革道路，但不是社会民主主义，而是社会主义的自我完善。

○ 我们党的优点是没有社会民主主义的影响，十年改革是有成绩的，否则不可能抵御这次全世界的动乱。

- 高等学校是重灾区，坚持着作的只有1/3，相当比例的基层组织没有战斗力，卷入动乱。少数学校，如深圳大学是官办动乱，广东省已将校长撤了。
- 罗马尼亚事件以后，反动标语增加，苏联的变化，表面上平静，也有影响。
- 寒假中学生作社会调查是满意的，特别是物价，扫黄等，但对党风仍有不满。
- 党风问题要搞好，但不能借反腐败否定党的领导。
- 十年舆论导向有问题。
- 否定毛泽东思想就是否定中共的历史。苏联是全盘否定斯大林。
- 去年政治上打了个大胜仗，经济，思想战线有转机，但不能期望很快改变局面，要很长的时间。
- 国内物价的下降，穿的上升。工业生产有困难，消费基金，集团购买力压了很多。江西省公费请客就下降了88%。目前市场疲软，产品积压，一汽积压了三万辆汽车。但农业去年比前年好。
- 全国停工3.5%，部分人要回农村去。机电业困难最大。

二 对美，加国学人员的方针和使领馆的指示

- 对留学生的工作要提到国际斗争和争夺人才的高度。要高举爱国主义的旗帜，揭露和打击少数人。争夺人才的斗争是长期的。驻外人员在第一线是很艰苦的，现在是关系命运的斗争，每个馆，每个人处于独立作战，许多事来不及请示就做，是允许的。
- 美国把留学生当人质，我们不能把留学生推过去。使馆人员要从斗争角度认识这个问题，不能只限于管理。
- 要留学生都回国来是不可能的，要实事求是，发展进步力量，团结中间派，孤立反动派。斗争要有理，有利，有节。现在在某种情况下有点象地下党，美国党组织不能公开。
- 留学生有爱国的，但不懂得爱社会主义，要正确对待，作艰苦的工作，也要看到希望，国家形势在好转。
- 要壮大第一类人员队伍，爱护他们，只有百分之几也要支持。正确对待动摇者，同反政府区别开来，骨干队伍分两种，一是始终坚定的，一是晃过一下的。
- 对第二，三类，包括一部份第四类，要用政策体现。在护照问题上树几个标兵。
- 打击对立面要作到心中有数，对于隐蔽的，不要急于打击。打击要分步骤，先打击连美国正直的

人也不齿的。

- 美国的教训是党的工作做晚了。坚定的组织起来，不坚定的保持联系，反动的清除。做到大部分爱国，争取一部分回国，其正坚持社会主义的，那怕百分之几也是好的。
- 要着力争取中间群众，口号、白话要适当。不要说多数留学生对祖国没有感情，他只是想多留一段时间，多赚一点钱，而全美学自联利用了这一点，对他们要宣传爱国主义。
- 留学生中抓好两头：党组织的建设和联谊会的作用，反对学自联，民阵，民联的活动。
- 要用两个调子讲话。公开讲爱国守法。对党员骨干还要讲社会主义，共产主义。有些骨干放到第三线，不公开活动，随时准备替换第二线的。
- 要搞些中间组织，如俱乐部，娱乐性活动，调子不要太高，团结争取中间偏我的。
- 对外宣布时讲，不是要求留学生回国服务，不是不要你们了。各种原因暂不回去，可以理解，时间不够可以延长，有困难的也可以帮助，相信大多数是爱国的，回国我们欢迎，留下也不催你回去。然后再处理几个延长护照等案例，就有影响了。
- 有人从J-1改为F-1，可按自费留学生对待。但要加以区别，有人可以更换护照，如愿意偿还培养费，我们欢迎，不还也不勉强，不计较这类小事。不还是欠了我们人情。要说明是非问题，还与不还都不对。少数人（约10%）的护照要个案处理。对反动骨干取消留学资格，开除党籍，开除国内公职，不准回国。多数人还是爱国的，对国家有感情的，长远会起作用的。在西方日子也不好过。
- 骗了民的，用行动改正了（回国），不予追究。
- 美加暂停派遣公派研究生，只派访问学者。在职人员配偶探亲，如单位不同意，可按退职处理，不要叫除名。留学生如果有5%回国，超过100%，这5%是火里炼出来的。
- 第一类留学生要作工作，希望都回来。我们还要与学术前沿保持接触。回来的人安置工作要作好，今后不再派这些年轻人了。36所院校出去了7000人，工作受到影响。
- 不先留土就留洋，不了解中国国情，这种做法不对，造成国内招研究生困难。由于"五年"规定，很多人不读研究生了，他们为留洋而读，干脆别招了。要宣布先留土，后留洋，或者只留土，不留洋。
- 大学毕业送出国学社会科学是不成功的，不过对留学生要讲，如果能结合中国国情，爱国爱社会主义，回来还是有用的。

o 学自联问题很复杂，要仔细研究。如宣布为反动组织，广大成员如何处理？现在不宣布是反动组织，但要打击坏头头。不能掌握在他们手中。

o 一月七日，公安部宣布吊销万润南，陈一谘，严家其等人护照。其他民联，民阵及学自联头头约100多人，与公安，外交部商定，分期分批吊销。主要是：1）以推翻社会主义，颠覆政府为目标的头面人物，民阵，民联及民主党的核心人物；2）煽动暴乱，策划及组织出席美国合听证会及提供材料的为首分子；3）公开要求政治避难者；4）坚持反政府，反党，在公开场合鼓吹反党论调的报刊，电台主要负责人；5）与国内外反华反共势力勾结，串联，筹款情节恶劣者。第一批先打击1）中五，六人，横人格差的，如吾尔开希。

o 关于全美学自联的国会游说活动，要说多数人是为了留下来而卷入，可以理解。但要严格处理为首者如刘永川，郭联洞等。

o 打击几个人的问题，要起个名目，抗战时期叫"汉奸"，我们要想个叫得响的名称，不能叫"持不同政见者"。

o 在我们政策作出符合实际的调整以后，争取更多留学生团结在我们周围，以防美国再来一手。这个政策是根据留学生力量对比制定的，无非是争取中间，打击一头，巩固一头。

三 留学生中党组织的工作

o 组织立场坚定的党员过组织生活，3--5人一组，条件不成熟的也可以单线联系。认识模糊的要排定党员联系，继续考查，如不行先挂起来。

o 取得居留权的党员（主要在加拿大）只要爱国，党籍留不处理，算作特殊党员。接受西方观念而公开反党者，开除党籍。

o 违反原则，串联退党的要开除。国外要按具体情况办，本人要退，查实后可同意。一时不明真相，受到蒙蔽，事后彻回退党要求的，可分别处理，给处分或留党察看。本人不知道，别人代签的不算退党。

o 加强组织建设，清的清，退的退，把表现好的组织起来，也可以单线联系。党员出国前要培训，所有关系都转使领馆。

o 81年已有文件，长期不回国的停止党籍，统计党员时另算。公派人员不与我联系，一年不交党费作自行退党处理。

- 党组织的存在是为了斗争，在斗争中保持活力。只有党组织工作做好了，留学生工作才能作好。美加党组织瓦解了，党组织活动不容在了，但党员还在。有人为了改造党才入党，这不叫共产党员。

- 我们的工作第一步是掌握党组织，第二步是抓联谊会。要求不能太紧太高。按地下党办法，每校有几名可靠的，成立小支部，骨干可以让留下来。

四. 中美，中加关系

- 奥森伯格来华谈判恢复富布赖特交流计划时提，美国人也不希望中国学生起哄。

- "六四"后中美关系进入低潮，现在差不多到了谷底。美方对解严，放人反映不强烈，只是一般欢迎。人权报告出来后，关系又复紧张。中美关系在短期内不可能好转。

- 美欧策过去是两党一致，现在分两派。一派认为，中国失去或减弱了三大角中的地位，中国现代化要资金，技术，有求于美国，制裁可以压中国就范，目前中国改革在倒退。另一派认为，压和拉要结合，中国的三角地位下降，战略地位仍不容忽视，对苏牵制，西亚地区也有影响，所以得保持对话，遏贷"六四"的同时，使中国回到改革之路。这也是布什的观点。但底线是不能超越"六四"。

- 布什的观点是：1）维持现状；2）保持压力；3）留有余地。两派的目的是一致的。形势估计上不同。我们可以利用矛盾，布什在留学生问题上是压，卫星问题上是拉。

- 留学生问题取决于内部因素，也有国际因素。对外解释讲得圆满一点。对美加政府都要施加压力。我们抗议美国的行政拖迟，按肯要再交涉。

- 美国手中有两张牌，人权报告及关于"五年"规定的报告；五月份又要讨论最惠国待遇。美国用留学生问题当作压中国的重磅炸弹。

- 我们手里的牌不多，富布赖特交流计划是一张，继续派留学生，和平队以及放人问题。我们是弯弓不发，让美国人摸不着头脑。对学自联头头的扣留和打击如能成功，是对美国政府的压力。

- 自费留学"五年"规定，只是内部宣布，击中美国要害，要坚持。"华声报"全文登了，公开出去也没关系。

o 美制裁不取消，中美关系不会有多大发展，留学生政策也不会改变。

o 加拿大移民问题要保持压力，由胶着，对华秋贷资交涉，暂时停派人赴加，但不是长远之计。

  美加不同，美希望留学生回国发挥作用，加是搞移民，掠夺人才，今后要同加签个协定。

o 美国在苏联如果得手，对中国压力还会加大。

Appendix 2
Translation

(Directive on Policy toward Chinese Students and Scholars in the United States and Canada, March, 1990)

The original Chinese text of the summary appears at the end of this translation.

At the moment, our country has more than 50,000 students and scholars in the United States and Canada. Overseas students are facing an extremely serious and complicated situation. It has become a fierce political struggle and a struggle over human talents. The American Administration has completely accepted the four provisions of the Congress, "The Emergency Immigration Relief Act of 1989 for Chinese Nationals," exempting tens of thousands of our students and scholars holding J-1 visas from their obligations to return to serve China. The Canadian Government, in order to plunder our human talents, has changed its normal immigration procedures and, using "special case handling," is encouraging a huge number of our students and scholars to become immigrants (reportedly, about 6,000 people have applied for and started the immigration procedure). Such rude interference by the American and Canadian Governments in our country's internal affairs, their rampant act of plundering our human talents, their years of ideological infiltration and corruption of our students and scholars abroad, and their implementation of the strategy of "peaceful evolution" have made an enormous impact on the changes of the thinking of our overseas students and scholars and the division among them. About 70-80 percent of the total number of our government-sponsored students and scholars in the United States and Canada will not return to China in the near future, or will stay there for a long period of time or immigrate to foreign countries. About 10 percent of our students and scholars actively participate in activities against our government, in an attempt to establish a bourgeois republic. On the other hand, those who have relatively high political-ideological awareness, a relatively high degree of patriotism and are our core elements there account for less than 5 percent of the total number of students.

1. The Working Principles On Chinese Students and Scholars in the United States and Canada:

Work from the perspective of international political struggle, hold high the banner of patriotism, intensify ideological and political work, rely on and strengthen our core forces, win over the majority, strike at the tiny minority of core anti-government activists.

Our work should proceed by adhering to the above principles. In the near future, the basic emphasis of our work overseas will not be on the issue of overseas students and scholars returning to China, but on the issue of whether they are patriotic or not.

We must fully recognize the necessity, the long-term nature and difficulty of counter-infiltration and counter-subversion.

2. The Specific Principles on different treatment of different Categories of Overseas Students and Scholars:

Summarizing the political positions of our overseas students and scholars, their attitudes toward our government, their attitudes toward the U.S. and Canadian administrative measures or immigration policies, and their demonstrated acts on the issue of returning to serve China, the government has classified five different categories and devised appropriate and differentiated measures in response.

First category: People in this category have a higher political awareness and a more correct position and understanding of anti-government activities. They do not accept the exemption [of two-year home residency requirement] or apply to become immigrants; they are willing to return to China or undertake the procedures of temporarily staying abroad according to the requirements of our government (embassies and consulates). We must firmly protect and support this group of people and, moreover, teach them how to be good at uniting the students and scholars in the middle so as to increase the forces we may rely upon. In the complex environment abroad, they may become targets. We must adopt firm measures to protect them. If they are unable to continue to study or work in the U.S. and Canada, we may transfer them to other countries or back in China to continue their studies. After they return to China, we will adopt appropriate measures of benefits for them on issues like job placement, scientific research conditions, professional evaluation, household registration, housing and opportunities to go abroad again. Some of them may, according to our needs, continue to stay abroad to study or work in order to give full play to their political role and their role of uniting and organizing overseas students and scholars.

Second category: People in this category have some patriotism and hope their socialist motherland will prosper and become strong. But in the near future these people will not fully agree with our government's principles and policies. But they do not oppose our government from a fundamental political perspective. They can maintain ties with our embassies and consulates. From the perspective of their personal interest, they do not plan to return to China in the near future. Some will stay abroad for a long time or even apply to become immigrants, but have not decided whether to become citizens of foreign countries. We should, taking into account practical circumstances, adopt a tolerant attitude toward such people, continue to maintain ties with them, allow them to extend their duration of studies and work abroad, and permit them to enjoy the benefits of overseas students and scholars. When people in this category apply to our government to change their passports to those issued for private affairs, if they offer to pay back the expenses related to their overseas studies, we may accept. If they are unable to pay back these expenses for certain reasons, they need to explain the circumstances to our embassies and consulates abroad and fill out "Forms for Changing Passports." Their applications may be processed. We may explain to our government-sponsored students in other countries that those whom the government has sponsored for fewer than two years is to avoid a chain reaction.

Third category: People in this category are ideologically more deeply influenced by Western values and hold politically different views about our principles and policies; they do not plan to return to serve the country. But they do not yet belong to the group of people who actively participate in activities against our government. Some of them have already changed their visa categories or obtained permanent residence rights, and may gain foreign citizenship in three to five years. We still need to educate and win over people in this category and point out that it is a mistake for them to receive, without our authorization, the U.S. or Canada's special exemption or immigration measures. But they may still be treated as self-sponsored overseas students and scholars. When people in this category apply to our government to change their passports to the classification of for-private affairs, their cases may be handled in the same way as the people in the Second category. After they have explained the circumstances to our embassies and consulates and filled out "Forms for Changing Passports," their applications for for-private-affairs passports may also be processed.

Fourth category: These are activists who have actively participated in anti-government activities. We must conduct criticism, education and necessary reasoned struggles against these people, adopting the policy of dividing and splitting them. When we handle their applications for passport extensions or related matters, we must impose strict control. After they have changed their attitudes, their cases may be handled individually. Their scholarships may be cut off. Moreover, we must demand that they pay back all the expenses related to their overseas studies and we must also stop their benefits as overseas students and scholars, and, impose necessary restrictions on their return to China and on their families' visits abroad. For those in this category who have truly demonstrated their repentance, they may be treated as people in the third category.

Fifth category: These are reactionary core elements who actively organize and plan anti-government activities. They are the targets for us to expose and strike at. At appropriate moments, we should single out their influential leaders who have committed extremely vile acts to expose and attack them publicly. At the moment, we must first attack the small number of evil leaders of the "U.S. Independent Federation of Chinese Students and Scholars" and "Canadian Federation of Chinese Students and Scholars" like Liu Yongchuan, Han Liangchao, Xu Bangtai and Qu Xiaohua. When concrete evidence is obtained, their status as overseas students and scholars must be revoked.; they are to be ordered to pay back all the expenses related to overseas studies. Their applications for passport extensions must be refused. We can cancel the passports of some of them. They will not be allowed to return to China before they abandon their anti-government position and commit concrete acts of repentance. They are to be fired by their previous employers, and their families must be banned from visiting them abroad.

The general principle is: rely on and increase our core forces (the first category), unite and win over the majority (the second and third categories), divide and split those who have participated in anti-government activities (the fourth category), ruthlessly expose and strike at the tiny number of core anti-government elements (the fifth category).

3. On the Construction of the Communist Party Organization and Handling of Communist Party Members:

We need to conduct a thorough examination and investigation of the Party organizations and the conditions of Party members, and adopt appropriate responsive measures to deal with different situations:

(1) Those Partymembers who have steadfast political positions and firmly believe in Communism should, according to the situation of struggle, be organized in different forms (generally we may use the form of policy and situation study groups). The activities of the Party organizations should be mainly small-scale and dispersed; moreover, the secret forms of struggle should, be adopted to give full play to their political and organizations roles and use them as the core to unite and win over the majority of the overseas students and scholars.

(2) Those Party members with fuzzy understanding, wavering political positions, serious individualistic ideas but have not yet fallen to the side of the anti-Party and anti-government force to be won over, by using the method of single-individual contact from the protective layer for our core elements. Moreover, they need to be continually monitored and tested in actual struggles.

(3) Those Party members who have gained permanent residence rights abroad (including the status of immigrants) may tem-

porarily still have their Party membership maintained if their political attitudes are relatively good, if they show good feeling toward the motherland and have done something that benefits the government. We will appoint special personnel to maintain contact with them.

(4) Those Party members who have lost their Communist beliefs and have completely accepted bourgeois values, as long as they do not engage in anti-Party and anti-government activities must have their ties with the Party organizations cut off at the moment. Those who have offered to withdraw from the Party may be treated as such. Those who openly engage in anti-Party and anti-government activities must be expelled from the Party without exception.

4. Adjustment of our policy of sending students to the United States and Canada in response to the situations there. Due to the U.S. and Canadian Government's policies toward our overseas students and scholars and their plundering of our human talents, we must exert pressures on the U.S. and Canadian Governments and respond with further reactions to wage a struggle in response. The following measures are to be adopted:

(1) Stop sending government-sponsored degree-candidate graduate students to the United States and Canada.

(2) The visiting-scholars sent (to these countries) must be politically mature and reliable, over a relatively long period of time. At the same time, the number is to be reduced.

(3) Family members within China who want to go to visit the students and scholars in the U.S. and Canada are to be restricted to family members of only those who are studying for degrees abroad and have spent more than a year abroad. The persons to be visited are limited to only the spouses of the family members within China. If the persons to be visited are placed in the fourth category listed above, and if their spouses are employed in China, severe restrictions are to be placed on them. If the persons to be visited belong in the fifth category, travel permission is denied.

目前，我在美国和加拿大有留学人员五万多名，留学工作面临十分严峻和复杂

的形势，已成为一场激烈的政治斗争和争夺人才的斗争。美国政府全盘接受国会《19

89年紧急放宽中国移民法案》的四项内容，豁免我数万名持J-1签证的留学人员回国

服务的义务；加拿大政府为了掠夺我人才，改变了正常的移民程序，按"特殊案例"策

动我大批留学人员移民（据悉，已申办移民手续的有六千人左右）。美、加当局这种

粗暴干涉我国内政、肆意掠夺我人才的举动和长期以来对我留学人员思想上的渗透、

腐蚀及"和平演变"战略的实施，对我留学人员思想的变化和队伍的分化产生了重

大影响：约占美、加地区公派留学人员总数百分之七十至八十的人近期不会回国，

或长期滞留，或移民国外；积极参与反对我政府活动的留学人员约占百分之十左右；

反政府核心骨干分子约百余人，这些人与美国、加拿大右翼反共势力、台湾反动势

力和国内逃亡分子相互勾结，策划和组织反对我政府的活动，妄图建立资产阶级共

和国；而政治思想觉悟较高，有较强爱国心的留学生骨干不足总数的百分之五。

一．对在美、加留学人员的工作方针

学习或工作，以发挥他们的政治作用和团结、组织留学人员的作用。

第二类：有爱国心，希望社会主义祖国繁荣富强，但一个时期内会不完全同意我方针、政策，但不是在根本政治立场上反对我政府，能与我使、领馆保持联系。他们从个人利益出发，近期不打算回国，有的会较长期留在国外，甚至申请移民，但未决定是否要加入外国国籍的人员。对他们要从实际情况出发，采取宽容的态度，继续与之保持联系，同意延长其在国外的学习和工作期限，享受留学人员的待遇。这类人员向我申办更换因私普通护照时，如提出偿还出国留学费用，可以接受。若因某种原因不能偿还时，向我驻外使、领馆说明情况，填写《更换护照申请表》，可为其办理。对在其他国家的我公派留学生可以说明，国家资助两年以下费用的，一般可以从宽，不归还。以免引起连锁反应。

第三类：在思想上受西方的价值观念影响较深，在政治上对我方针、政策持不同意见，不打算回国服务，但尚不属于积极参与反对我国政府活动的人员。这些人中的一部分已改变签证种类或已取得永久居留权，三、五年内可能加入外国国籍。对这类人员仍要立足于教育和争取，指出其擅自接受美国或加拿大的特殊豁免或移民措施是错误的，但仍可视为自费留学人员予以对待。这类人员向我申办更换因私普通护照时，可按第二类人员处理，在其向我驻外使、领馆说明情况，填写《更换护照申请表）后，亦可为其办理因私普通护照。

第四类：积极参与反政府活动分子。对这些人要进行批评教育和必要的说理斗争，采取分化瓦解的政策。在办理护照延长等事宜时，要从严掌握，在其改变态度后，个案处理。可停止他们的奖学金，并要提出偿还出国留学的一切费用的要求，不给于留学人员的待遇。对其回国和家属探亲加以必要限制。对其中确有悔改表现者，可按第三类人员对待。

第五类：积极组织、策划反政府活动的反动骨干分子。他们是揭露和打击的对象。要在适当的时机选择其中影响大，情节恶劣的为首分子进行公开的揭露和打击。当前，首先打击"全美学自联"和"全加学联"等组织的少数坏头头，如刘永川、韩联潮、徐邦泰、瞿晓铧等。在证据确凿的情况下，取消其留学人员的资格，责令其偿还一切出国留学费用，不为其办理延长护照有效期，有的可吊销其护照。在不放弃反政府立场和无悔改的实际行动前不许他们回国，由原单位开除公职，不允其家属探亲。

总的原则是：要依靠、壮大骨干队伍（第一类），团结争取大多数（第二、三类），分化瓦解参与反政府活动的人员（第四类），并狠狠揭露和打击极少数反政府的骨干分子（第五类）。

三．关于党的组织建设及党员处理

要对党组织和党员情况进行认真的摸底和调查，分别不同情况，采取相应的措

施:

1.对政治立场坚定、坚信共产主义的党员，要根据斗争的形势，以各种不同的形式(一般可用政策形势学习小组形式)把他们组织起来，党组织的活动以小型分散为主，且采取秘密的斗争方式，发挥他们的政治、组织作用，作为团结和争取广大留学人员的核心；

2.对于认识模糊，立场动摇，个人主义思想严重，但未滑到反党、反政府势力方面去的党员，可采取单线联系的做法，作为骨干力量的外围予以争取，并继续在实际斗争中加以考察和考验；

3.对于在外取得永久居留权(含移民)的党员，如果他们政治态度较好，与祖国有感情并做了一些对国家有利的事情，则目前暂不作党籍处理，由我指定专人与之联系；

4.对已丧失共产主义信仰，全盘接受资产阶级价值观的党员，只要他们不从事反党、反政府的活动，目前要切断他们与党组织的联系。对其中提出退党的，可按退党处理。对于公开从事反党、反政府活动的，则一律开除出党。

四、针对美、加情况调整派遣政策

鉴于美、加政府对我留学人员的政策和对我人才的掠夺，要对美、加政府施加压力，作出进一步反应，进行相应的斗争。要采取以下措施：

1.停止派遣赴美、加公派攻读研究生学位的留学人员；

2.派出的访问学者必须是政治上成熟、可靠，并具有较丰富的实际工作经验，工作时间较长的人员。同时减少派出数量。

3.国内人员去往美、加地区对留学人员探亲，一般限于已在国外攻读研究生学位和时间在一年以上的留学人员。探亲对象仅限于国内人员的配偶。如探亲对象属于上述第四类人员，其配偶属于在职人员，则应从严掌握；属第五类人员的，可不予批准。

Notes

Chapter 1 Introduction

1. Giles, *Sun Tzu,* 194.
2. Kierman and Fairbank, *Chinese Ways in Warfare,* 30-41.
3. Overend, "China Seen Using Close U.S. Ties," sec. 1, 34.
4. Ibid.

Chapter 2 Framework for Analysis

1. Barnett, *Cadres, Bureaucracy, and Political Power,* 450.

Chapter 3 China's Information Objectives

1. Source no. 1, interviewed 19 April 1992.
2. Lo Ping, "Unstable Regions Set Forth," 6-7.
3. PRC State Education Commission, *Summary of the Meeting of Educational Counselors* (see appendix 1).

Chapter 4 Organizational Structure

1. Richelson, *Foreign Intelligence Organizations,* 277.
2. Du Xichuan and Zhang Lingyuan, *China's Legal System,* 135.
3. Central Intelligence Agency, *Directory of Chinese Officials and Organizations,* 42.
4. *Who's Who in China,* 271.
5. Central Intelligence Agency, *Directory of Chinese Officials and Organizations,* 25-43.

6. Barnett, *Making of Foreign Policy,* 121.

7. Barnett, *Cadres, Bureaucracy, and Political Power,* 450.

8. Ibid., 12.

9. Ibid., 48.

10. Source no. 1, interviewed 19 April 1992.

11. Barnett, *Cadres, Bureaucracy, and Political Power,* 87.

12. Ibid., 88.

13. Barnett, *Making of Foreign Policy,* 90, 91.

14. Ibid., 90, 121.

15. Barnett, *Cadres, Bureaucracy, and Political Power,* 96-98.

16. Source no. 1, interviewed 18 March 1992.

17. Hong Kong AFP, "Intelligence Official's Defection Major Blow," K1.

18. Richelson, *Foreign Intelligence Organizations,* 299.

19. Hong Kong AFP, "Court Sentences Ex-Mainland Official to Prison," 42.

20. "PRC Spy Tung Li Sentenced to 12 Years in Taiwan," 1.

21. Hong Kong AFP, "Court Sentences Ex-Mainland Official to Prison," 42.

22. Hong Kong Zhongguo Xinwen She, "KMT Special Agent Sentenced to Prison in Wenzhou," K8.

23. Barnett, *Cadres, Bureaucracy, and Political Power,* 222-23.

24. Wise and Ross, *Espionage Establishment,* 189; Deacon, *Chinese Secret Service,* 319-20; Faligot and Kauffer, *Kang Shen and the Chinese Secret Service,* 402; Lamar, "Spies Everywhere," 30; Mary Thorton, "China Protests U.S. Expulsion," A20.

25. Barnett, *Making of Foreign Policy,* 90.

26. District Court, United States v. Chin, 4:106.

27. Barnett, *Cadres, Bureaucracy, and Political Power,* 98.

28. Richelson, *Foreign Intelligence Organizations,* 282.

29. Butterfield, *Alive in the Bitter Sea,* 334.

Chapter 5 Foreign Operations

1. Overend, "China Seen Using Close U.S. Ties," sec. 1, 34.

2. Senate Select Committee on Intelligence, *Meeting the Espionage Challenge,* 19.

3. Overend, "China Seen Using Close U.S. Ties," sec. 1, 34.

4. Joint Economic Committee of Congress, *China under the Four Modernizations,* 560.

5. Knight-Ridder News Service, "Chinese Stole U.S. Neutron Bomb Plans," A2.

6. San Jose Mercury News Service, "Chinese Stole Secret for Neutron Bomb," 38.

7. Faligot and Kauffer, *Kang Shen and the Chinese Secret Service,* 425.

8. Mecham, "Bush Overturns Sale," 34.

9. Auerbach, "President Tells China to Sell Seattle Firm," A3.

10. Central Intelligence Agency, *Military Organizations,* chart.

11. Senate Committee on Governmental Affairs, *Foreign Missions Act,* 98.

12. Department of Commerce, Bureau of Export Administration, *Action Affecting Export Privileges,* 6.

13. Department of Commerce, Bureau of Export Administration, *Denial Orders,* 3.

14. Ibid., supplement 2 to part 788, 7.

15. District Court, United States v. Chin, 1:1.

16. Ibid., 6:97.

17. Ibid., 4:12.

18. Ibid., 6:102-6.

19. Ibid., 3:45.

20. KGB transmission no. 11781/X, "Work on China," 5 June 1985, in Andrew and Gordievsky, *Instructions from the Centre,* 208.

21. KGB transmission no. 822/PR/62, "Work on China," 13 September 1976, in ibid., 195.

22. Source no. 1, interviewed 18 March 1992.

23. District Court, United States v. Chin, 4:85, 153, 106.

24. Campbell, "Sources of Information."

25. District Court, United States v. Chin, 3:56.

26. Army Intelligence Center and School, *Counterintelligence,* 103, 3, 14.

27. District Court, United States v. Chin, 3:112-13.

28. Ibid., 3:22, 105.

29. Source no. 2, interviewed 13 May 1992.

30. District Court, United States v. Chin, supplement 1 to vol. 2, 112.

31. Ibid., 3:22.

32. Wise and Ross, *Espionage Establishment,* 198; Wills and Moskin, *Turncoat,* 151.

33. Wills and Moskin, *Turncoat,* 151.

34. Wise and Ross, *Espionage Establishment,* 198.

35. Ibid.

36. Shenon, "Two Chinese Depart in Espionage Case," A1.

37. "Chinese Reportedly Tried to Get American to Spy," A35.

38. Pear, "Chinese in U.S. Report Harassment," A7.

39. Source no. 3.

40. Lu, "Spying Admission Stuns Group," sec. 2, 1.

41. House Committee on the Post Office and Civil Service, *Mail Interruption,* 36-37.

42. Asia Watch, *Punishment Season,* 55-56.

43. Source no. 1, interviewed 18 March 1992.

44. Source no. 3.

45. Oberdorfer, "Chinese Envoy Asks Political Asylum," A9.

46. Xu Lin, testimony before the House Foreign Affairs Committee, *Alleged Intimidation and Harassment,* 1.

47. Ibid., 40, 41.

48. PRC State Education Commission, *Summary of the Meeting of Educational Counselors,* 6.

49. Gertz, "Chinese Diplomat Denounces Li," A5.

50. Xu Lin, testimony before the House Foreign Affairs Committee, *Alleged Intimidation and Harassment,* 5.

51. PRC State Education Commission, *Summary of the Meeting of Educational Counselors,* 2-4.

52. Ibid., 1, 5.

53. Source no. 1, interviewed 4 September 1992.

54. Xu Lin, testimony before the House Foreign Affairs Committee, *Alleged Intimidation and Harassment,* 3.

55. Source no. 3.

56. Source no. 4; source no. 1, interviewed 4 September 1992.

Chapter 6 Domestic Operations

1. Butterfield, *Alive in the Bitter Sea,* 40, 41, 323.

2. Ibid., 322.

3. Source no. 1, interviewed 18 March 1992; Du Xichuan and Zhang Lingyuan, *China's Legal System,* 133-34.

4. Butterfield, *Alive in the Bitter Sea,* 471-72; source no. 1, interviewed 2 May 1992.

5. Cheung, "Big Brother Is Watching," 24.

6. Butterfield, *Alive in the Bitter Sea,* 458.

7. Source no. 1, interviewed 2 May 1992; "World Politics and Current Affairs," 38.

8. Butterfield, *Alive in the Bitter Sea,* 472.

9. Ibid., 471.

10. Barnett, *Cadres, Bureaucracy, and Political Power,* 223.

11. Ibid.; Richelson, *Foreign Intelligence Organizations,* 277. Source no. 1 identified this unit as the General Staff's Third Department, while Richelson called it their technical department.

12. Ibid.

13. Source no. 1, interviewed 2 May 1992.

14. Source no. 1, interviewed 18 March 1992; Du Xichuan and Zhang Lingyuan, *China's Legal System,* 135.

15. Du Xichuan and Zhang Lingyuan, *China's Legal System,* 132-34.

16. Cheung, "Big Brother Is Watching," 24, 25.

17. Proceedings of the second annual Staunton Hill Conference on China's People's Liberation Army, 12.

18. Du Xichuan and Zhang Lingyuan, *China's Legal System,* 135.

19. "Resistance Toward Peaceful Evolution" (lecture).

20. Beijing Central Administrative Office, cable to Lhasa Ministry of State Security, Working Group, 4 March 1986.

21. Ibid.

22. Ibid.

23. Compiled from the debriefing reports of twenty-one refugees who claimed exposure to, or knowledge of, the use of informants in Tibet by the PRC.

24. Debriefing report of a layperson from Qinghai, former police officer Tamting Tsering, age 43.

25. Ibid.

26. Debriefing report of a layperson from Lhasa, former police officer Dawa Tsering, age 28.

27. Debriefing report of a layperson from Lhasa, former cadre Kelsang Namgyel, age 33.

28. Ibid.

29. Ibid.

30. Debriefing report of a layperson from Lhasa, former police officer Dawa Tsering, age 28.

31. Sun, "Dissident Struggle Still Alive," A21.

32. Hewitt, "Great Escape from China," D1.

33. Ibid., D2.

34. "Beijing Admits Gathering Information on Residents," 1.

35. Hong Kong Ming Pao, "Further on Security Minister Comments," 2.

36. Hewitt, "Great Escape from China," D2.

37. For example, see Sampson, "Peking Keeps Tabs on Foreign Spies"; Sun, "Foreign Press Pressed by Chinese System," A27; Baum, "Beijing's Stricter Eye on Foreigners," 1.

38. Sun, "Foreign Press Pressed by Chinese System," A32.

39. Sampson, "Peking Keeps Tabs on Foreign Spies."

40. Sun, "Foreign Press Pressed by Chinese System," A27, 32.

41. Ibid., A32.

42. Butterfield, *Alive in the Bitter Sea,* 33, 34; Southerland, "How China Watches China Watchers," C2.

43. Rudolph, Cankao Xiaoxi. Rudolph's work is an in-depth review of two hundred issues of *Reference News.* He identifies frequent instances of censorship, omissions, and mistranslations, all of which seem designed to support PRC propaganda positions.

44. Schlesinger, "China Plans Build-Up of Spy Network."

45. Source no. 1, interviewed 2 May 1992.

46. Gertz, "Sex Is Old Angle in Spying Game," A4.

47. Butterfield, *Alive in the Bitter Sea,* 33, 34; Southerland, "How China Watches China Watchers," C2.

48. Butterfield, *Alive in the Bitter Sea,* 33, 34.

49. Source no. 1, interviewed 24 July 1992.

50. Kristof, "Enemies Are Everywhere," D1.

Chapter 7 Agent Recruitment Methods

1. For example, see Tennien, *No Secret Is Safe,* 158; Watt, China Spy, 138.

2. Source no. 1, interviewed 2 May 1992.

3. Ibid.

4. Butterfield, *Alive in the Bitter Sea,* 472.

5. For example, see Sampson, "Peking Keeps Tabs on Foreign Spies," 1; Sun, "Foreign Press Pressed by Chinese System," A27; Baum, "Beijing's Stricter Eye on Foreigners," 1.

6. Sampson, "Peking Keeps Tabs on Foreign Spies," 1.

7. Baum, "Beijing's Stricter Eye on Foreigners," 1.

8. Deacon, *Chinese Secret Service,* 402, 403.

9. "Chinese Reportedly Tried to Get American to Spy," A35.

10. Kristof, "Enemies Are Everywhere," 59.

11. Butterfield, *Alive in the Bitter Sea,* 471; source no. 1, interviewed 2 May 1992; Lu, "Spying Admission Stuns Group," sec. 2, 1.

12. Butterfield, "Chinese in the U.S.," A22.

13. KGB cable no. 1, no. 822/PR/62, "On Certain National-Psychological Characteristics of the Chinese, and Their Evaluation in the Context of Intelligence Work," 13 September 1976, in Andrew and Gordievsky, *Instructions from the Centre,* 194-95.

14. "Activist Claims Chinese Forced Him to Spy," 1.

15. District Court, United States v. Chin, 2:56.

16. Source no. 1, interviewed 18 March 1992; source no. 2, interviewed 13 May 1992.

17. Source no. 2, interviewed 13 May 1992.

18. Ibid. The following account is based on this interview.

19. Butterfield, "China to Let Fewer Students Go Abroad," A5.

20. Central Intelligence Agency, *World Factbook 1990,* 64.

21. Fox example, see "Activist Claims Chinese Forced Him to Spy," 1; Lu, "Spying Admission Stuns Group," sec. 2, 1.

22. Source no. 1, interviewed 2 May 1992.

23. Ibid.

24. U.S. Congress, *Immigration Status of Chinese Nationals,* 201-8.

25. Source no. 1, interviewed 18 March 1992; "Activist Claims Chinese Forced Him to Spy," 1; Lu, "Spying Admission Stuns Group," sec. 2, 1.

26. "Activist Claims Chinese Forced Him to Spy," 1; Lu, "Spying Admission Stuns Group," sec. 2, 1.

27. Ibid.

28. "Activist Claims Chinese Forced Him to Spy," 1.

29. "Activist Claims Chinese Forced Him to Spy," 1; Lu, "Spying Admission Stuns Group," sec. 2, 1.

30. Source no. 1, interviewed 18 March 1992; source no. 9; PRC State Education Commission, *Summary of the Meeting of Educational Counselors,* 5.

31. Beijing Central Administrative Office, cable to Lhasa Ministry of State Security, Working Group, 4 March 1986.

32. Law Association for Asia and the Pacific Human Rights Standing Committee, *Defying the Dragon,* 64.

33. Ibid.

34. Hoang Huan, "Build a Firm and Strong Border Line," 127.

35. For example, see Hai Au, "Mine Explosion by Chinese Henchmen Exposed," 51; "Aid Worker to Learn of Possible Dismissal," 1.

36. Stroud, "Why I Spoke Out," 15.

37. For example, see Hoang Huan, "Build a Firm and Strong Border Line," 121; Minh Nguyen, "Exhibition On Maintenance of Politico-Economic Security," 144, 145; "Enticing People to Engage in Sabotage," 211.

38. Hoang Huan, "Build a Firm and Strong Border Line," 121-22.

39. Overend, "China Seen Using Close U.S. Ties," sec. 1, 33.

Chapter 8 Military Intelligence Department

1. Source no. 1, interviewed 18 March 1991; source no. 5.

2. Godwin, *Development of the Chinese Armed Forces,* 41.

3. Swaine, *Military and Political Succession,* 255.

4. *Who's Who in China,* 816-17.

5. Source no. 1, interviewed 2 May 1992.

6. Source no. 1, as described in 1990 by Li Ning, Second Department intelligence officer and former PRC military attaché to the United Kingdom.

7. Johns Hopkins University, Student Locator Service, contacted by telephone by the author, May 1992.

8. Kent, *Strategic Intelligence for American World Policy,* 32-38.

9. Chen, "PRC in Dilemma over Expulsion," 4.

10. Ibid.; source no. 1, interviewed 2 May 1992; source no. 5.

11. Source no. 1, interviewed 18 March 1992.

12. Richelson, *Sword and Shield,* 41.

Chapter 9 Departmental Structure

1. International Institute for Strategic Studies, *Military Balance,* 1989-1990, 144-48.

2. Hong Kong Tangtai, "China Gathers Military Intelligence in Hong Kong," 86.

3. Defense Intelligence Agency, *Handbook of the Chinese People's Liberation Army,* 33, 34.

4. Ibid., 33; "Amphibious Zhongdui Trains Special Forces Troops," 86.

5. Godwin, *Development of the Chinese Armed Forces,* 86-88.

6. Defense Intelligence Agency, *Handbook of the Chinese People's Liberation Army,* 33.

7. Source no. 8.

8. Godwin, *Development of the Chinese Armed Forces,* 38-40.

9. Defense Intelligence Agency, *Handbook of the Chinese People's Liberation Army,* 33.

10. Source no. 8.

11. Ibid.; source no. 5. It should be noted that there were slight differences in the information reported by these sources. These differences involved the numerical designations of the Second Department's bureaus. Both sources acknowledged that numerous structural changes are occurring within PLA intelligence as a result of the 14th Party Congress. The following account is based on these reports.

12. Barnett, *Making of Foreign Policy in China,* 124.

13. Ibid., 125.

14. Source no. 5.

15. "Society of Military Science Founded," 1.

16. *Liaowang,* 3.

17. "Society of Military Science Founded," 1.

18. *Liaowang,* 3.

19. "Society of Military Science Founded," 1.

20. Source no. 5; source no. 8.

21. Ibid.

22. Ibid.

23. Ibid.

24. Source no. 7.

25. Source no. 5.

26. Ibid.

27. Ibid.; source no. 6.

28. Source no. 7; Godwin, *Development of the Chinese Armed Forces,* 62.

29. Godwin, *Development of the Chinese Armed Forces*, 41.
30. Ibid., 62.
31. Ibid.
32. Dornan and de Lee, *Chinese War Machine*, 74.
33. Defense Intelligence Agency, *People's Liberation Army Air Force*, 6-4.
34. Godwin, *Development of the Chinese Armed Forces*, 40-41.
35. Defense Intelligence Agency, *People's Liberation Army Air Force*, 6-1.
36. Ibid., 6-2.
37. Ibid.
38. Ibid., 6-3.
39. Ibid.
40. Ibid.; source no. 7; Godwin, *Development of the Chinese Armed Forces*, 40. In 1985 Godwin identified the Liaison Department by its former name, the Enemy Affairs Department.
41. Source no. 7; Dornan and de Lee, *Chinese War Machine*.
42. Defense Intelligence Agency, *People's Liberation Army Air Force*, 6-4.
43. Ibid., 6-5.
44. Source no. 7.
45. Source no. 8; "Secret Paper Describes Myriad Problems in PLA," 98.
46. Ibid., 100.

Chapter 10 Military Intelligence Operations

1. Defense Intelligence Agency, *Handbook of the Chinese People's Liberation Army*, 33.
2. Praval, *Indian Army after Independence*, 185.
3. Rowland, *History of Sino-Indian Relations*, 129-32.
4. "Communique Describes PRC Crimes Against Cao Bang," 45-46.
5. Ibid.; Duong Quyen, "Recognize the Enemy," 27.
6. Defense Intelligence Agency, *Handbook of the Chinese People's Liberation Army*, 35.
7. "Meo Vac Remains Firm," 42.
8. Hoang Huan, "Build a Firm and Strong Border Line," 121.
9. "Security in a Mountain District," 70.

10. Hoang Huan, "Build a Firm and Strong Border Line," 122.

11. Phong Vien, "Trial Reveals Beijing's Black Heart," 179; "Enticing People to Engage in Sabotage," 212; Do Quang, "Vigilantly Defend the Homeland," 159.

12. For example, see Thanh Binh, "Illegal Fishing Vessels," 54.

13. Defense Intelligence Agency, *Handbook of the Chinese People's Liberation Army,* 33; "Amphibious Zhongdui Trains Special Forces Troops," 86.

14. "Amphibious Zhongdui Trains Special Forces Troops," 86.

15. Ibid., 89.

16. Thanh Binh, "Illegal Fishing Vessels," 54.

17. "Communist China's New Taiwan Invasion Plan," 70.

18. "Communique Describes PRC Crimes Against Cao Bang," 46.

19. Ibid.; Dang Ngha, "Border Open-Air Market," 75.

20. Tran Thien Nhien, "From a News Conference to Court Trial," K2, 3.

21. Source no. 1, as described in 1990 by Li Ning, Second Department intelligence officer and former PRC military attaché to the United Kingdom; source no. 5; Chen, "PRC in Dilemma over Expulsion," 4.

22. Source no. 5; Chen, "PRC in Dilemma over Expulsion," 4.

23. Chen, "PRC in Dilemma over Expulsion," 4.

24. Ibid.; Thorton, "China Protests U.S. Expulsion," A20.

25. For a very good review of this case, see John Barron, *Breaking the Ring.*

26. Vitaly Yurchenko, former KGB officer, quoted on jacket of ibid.

27. Richelson, *Foreign Intelligence Organizations,* 277; source no. 1, interviewed 2 May 1992; source no. 5.

28. Central Intelligence Agency, *Directory of Chinese Officials: National-Level Organizations,* 98.

29. Watkin, "Man Linked to Chinese Diplomats Indicted."

30. Ibid.; Watkin, "Taiwanese Man Pleads Guilty."

31. Watkin, "Man Linked to Chinese Diplomats Indicted"; Watkin, "Plot to Export Missiles Alleged."

32. Watkin, "Grand Jury Said to Look at Businessman."

33. Watkin, "Man Linked to Chinese Diplomats Indicted.

34. Watkin, "Taiwanese Man Pleads Guilty."

35. Central Intelligence Agency, *Directory of Chinese Officials and Organizations,* 72.

36. State Department, *Diplomatic List,* February 1992, 14.

37. International Institute for Strategic Studies, *Military Balance,* 1989-1990, 144-48.

38. Ibid., 149.

39. Beichman, "Wary Eyes on Beijing's Rearmament," E3.

40. Source no. 5; source no. 1, as described in 1990 by Li Ning, Second Department intelligence officer and former PRC military attache to the United Kingdom.

41. Kan, *Chinese Missile and Nuclear Proliferation,* CRS-10, summary page.

42. Source no. 5.

43. Ibid.

44. Kan, *Chinese Missile and Nuclear Proliferation,* CRS-10 and summary page.

45. Source no. 1, as described in 1990 by Li Ning, Second Department intelligence officer and former PRC military attaché to the United Kingdom; source no. 5.

46. Kan, *Chinese Missile and Nuclear Proliferation,* CRS-2.

47. Wise and Ross, *Espionage Establishment,* 167.

48. Ibid., 164-70, 172.

49. "Rhodesia: Kaunda Gives Way," 5.

50. "Chinese Communist Angolan Activity," 6.

51. Kabul Domestic Service, "Kabul on Extent of PRC Interference," C1.

52. Abdul Ghafoor Jawshan, interviewed by Richard W. Marsh, Jr.

53. Kabul Bakhtar, "Bakhtar on PRC Aid to Counter-Revolution," C1; Kabul Domestic Service, "Kabul on Extent of PRC Interference," C1; Coll, "Anatomy of a Victory," A24.

54. Kabul Domestic Service, "Kabul on Extent of PRC Interference," C1.

55. Bavrov, "Kabul Press Conference Reveals PRC Interference," D1.

56. Abdul Ghafoor Jawshan, interviewed by Richard W. Marsh, Jr. Jawshan was able to identify only the caliber and intended role (e.g., antiaircraft, heavy machine gun) of the armament, not the actual Chinese designations. Based on his descriptions, which were corroborated by numerous FBIS reports, the equipment was identified in Dornan and de Lee, *Chinese War Machine,* 119, 120.

57. Ibid.

58. Ibid.

59. Vasilyev, "PRC `Overt Interference' in Afghanistan Hit," D1; Kabul Bakhtar, "Treacherous Activities of Maoist Group Cited," C1.

60. Kabul Bakhtar, "Collusion in Aiding Rebels Blasted," C3.

61. Kabul Domestic Service, "Kabul on Extent of PRC Interference," C1.

62. Vasilyev, "PRC `Overt Interference' in Afghanistan Hit," D1.

63. Kabul Domestic Service, "Kabul on Extent of PRC Interference," C1.

64. Abdul Ghafoor Jawshan, interviewed by Richard W. Marsh, Jr.

Chapter 11 Secondary Intelligence Organizations

1. Defense Intelligence Agency, *People's Liberation Army Air Force,* 6-4.

2. Source no. 7.

3. Ibid.

4. Ibid.

5. Hong Kong Tangtai, "China Gathers Military Intelligence in Hong Kong," 86.

6. Source no. 1, interviewed 19 April 1992; source no. 5.

7. Lewis, Hua Di, and Xue Litai, "Beijing's Defense Establishment," 88.

8. Source no. 1, interviewed 19 April 1992; Source no. 5.

9. Ibid.

10. Ibid.; source no. 8.

11. Lewis, Hua Di, and Xue Litai, "Beijing's Defense Establishment," 87, 93.

12. Source no. 1, interviewed 19 April 1992.

13. For example, see the cases United States v. Chipex, Inc., et al., Northern District of California, violation of the Export Administration Act (EAA), November 1983, and United States v. Man Chung Tong, Western District of Washington, violation of EAA, February 1984.

14. Source no. 1, interviewed 19 April 1992.

15. Hong Kong Ming Pao, "PRC Intelligence Research Focuses on Defense Strategy," W1.

16. Source no. 1, interviewed 2 May 1992.

17. Ibid.
18. Barnett, *Making of Foreign Policy,* 112-13.
19. Rudolph, *Cankao Xiaoxi,* 34-37.
20. Ibid., 112-30.
21. Ibid.
22. Butterfield, *Alive in the Bitter Sea,* 390.
23. Rudolph, *Cankao Xiaoxi,* 103-9.
24. Source no. 1, interviewed 19 April 1992.
25. Barnett, *Making of Foreign Policy,* 48.
26. Source no. 1, interviewed 19 April 1992.
27. Ibid., interviewed 18 March 1991; Cheung, "Big Brother Is Watching," 24.
28. Cheung, "Big Brother Is Watching," 24.
29. *Who's Who in China,* 550-51.
30. Cheung, "Big Brother Is Watching," 24.
31. Ibid.
32. Source no. 8.
33. Ibid.
34. Source no. 1, interviewed 2 May 1992.

Selected Bibliography

PRIMARY SOURCES

Abdul Ghafoor Jawshan, military attaché, Embassy of the Democratic Republic of Afghanistan, Washington, D.C. Interviewed by Richard W. Marsh, Jr., 31 March 1992.

"Amphibious Zhongdui Trains Special Forces Troops." *Jianchuan Zhishi*, in Joint Publications Research Service, JPRS-CAR-90-075, 10 October 1990.

Bavrov, Herman. "Kabul Press Conference Reveals PRC 'Interference'." *Tass,* 18 February 1985. FBIS-SOV-85-033, vol. 3, no. 33, 19 February 1985.

Beijing Central Administrative Office. Cable to Lhasa Ministry of State Security, Working Group, 4 March 1986. Translated by Tang Daxian in an unpublished document compiled by the Tibetan Information Network, London, 6 August 1990.

Beijing Xinhua Domestic Service. "Cases Involving Kuomindang Spies Cracked." Translated by the Foreign Broadcast Information Service. FBIS daily report—China, national affairs, 20 August 1990, FBIS-CHI-90-161.

Changsha Hunan Provincial Service. "Two Taiwan Spies Arrested in Hunan." Translated by the Foreign Broadcast Information Service. FBIS daily report—China, regional affairs, FBIS-CHI-90-131, 9 July 1990.

Chen, David. "PRC in Dilemma over Diplomat's Expulsion." Hong Kong *South China Morning Post,* 5 December 1987. FBIS daily report—China, FBIS-CHI-88-002, 5 January 1988.

"Communique Describes PRC Crimes Against Cao Bang." Hanoi International Service, 27 May 1984, in Joint Publications Research Service, JPRS-SEA-84-086, 12 June 1984.

"Communist China's New Taiwan Invasion Plan." *Chieh Fang,* no. 114, January 1988, in Joint Publications Research Service, JPRS-CAR-88-008, 1 March 1988.

Dang Ngha. "The Border Open-Air Market." *Quan Doi Nhan Dan,* 6 March 1983, in Joint Publications Research Service, JPRS-SEA-83-336.

Debriefing report of a layperson from Lhasa, former cadre Kelsang Namgyel, age 33. Interview conducted by the International Campaign for Tibet, 24 July 1992, in Katmandu, Nepal.

Debriefing report of a layperson from Lhasa, former police officer Dawa Tsering, age 28. Interview conducted by the International Campaign for Tibet, 25 July 1992, in Katmandu, Nepal.

Debriefing report of a layperson from Qinghai, former police officer Tamting Tsering, age 43. Interview conducted by the International Campaign for Tibet, 25 July 1992, in Katmandu, Nepal.

Debriefing reports of twenty-one refugees who claimed exposure to, or knowledge of, the use of informants in Tibet by the PRC. Interviews conducted by the International Campaign for Tibet on multiple occasions in June and July 1992 in Katmandu, Nepal.

Do Quang. "Vigilantly Defend the Security of the Homeland: Miss Hong's Meatroll Café." *Nhan Dan,* 18 March 1985, in Joint Publications Research Service, JPRS-SEA-85-078, 16 May 1985.

Duong Quyen. "Recognize the Enemy—Dead and Lost Horses." *Quan Doi Nhan Dan,* 18 November 1981, in Joint Publications Research Service, JPRS-SEA-82-034, 11 January 1982.

"Enticing People and Sending Them Back to Engage in Sabotage Activities." *Quan Doi Nhan Dan,* 6 March 1983, in Joint Publications Research Service, JPRS-83-348, 27 April 1983.

Hai Au. "Mine Explosion by Chinese Henchmen Exposed." *Quan Doi Nhan Dan,* 23 May 1984, in Joint Publications Research Service, JPRS-SEA-84-103, 19 July 1984.

Hoang Huan. "Build a Firm and Strong Border Line and Defeat the Enemy's Multifaceted War of Sabotage." *Quan Doi Nhan Dan,* 2 December 1984, in Joint Publications Research Service, JPRS-SEA-85-027, 11 February 1985.

Hong Kong AFP. "Convicted Kuomintang Spies Include U.S. Citizen." FBIS daily report—China, 25 August 1986.

———. "Court Sentences Ex-Mainland Official to Prison." FBIS daily report—China, FBIS-CHI-88-056, 22 March 1988.

————. "Hubei Court Sentences Taiwan Spy to Prison." Translated by the Foreign Broadcast Information Service. FBIS daily report— China, 24 September 1986.

————. "Intelligence Official's Defection Major Blow." FBIS daily report—China, 2 September 1986.

Hong Kong Ming Pao. "Further on Security Minister Comments." FBIS daily report—China, FBIS-CHI-92-063, 1 April 1992.

————. "PRC Intelligence Research Focuses on Defense Strategy." Translated by the Foreign Broadcast Information Service. FBIS-CHI-86-115, vol. 1, no. 115, 16 June 1986.

Hong Kong Tangtai. "China Gathers Military Intelligence in Hong Kong." FBIS daily report—China, FBIS-CHI-90-104, 30 May 1990.

Hong Kong Zhongguo Xinwen She. "KMT Special Agent Sentenced to Prison in Wenzhou." Translated by the Foreign Broadcast Information Service. FBIS daily report—China, 3 October 1988.

Kabul Bakhtar. "Bakhtar on PRC Aid to Counter-Revolution," 12 August 1984. FBIS-SOA-84-157, vol. 8, no. 157, 13 August 1984.

————. "Collusion in Aiding Rebels Blasted," 4 June 1984. FBIS-SOA-84-108, vol. 8, no. 108, 4 June 1984.

————. "Treacherous Activities of Maoist Group Cited," 17 July 1984. FBIS-SOA-84-138, vol. 8, no. 138, 17 July 1984.

Kabul Domestic Service. "Kabul on Extent of PRC Interference in DRA," 10 March 1985. Translated by the Foreign Broadcast Information Service. FBIS-SOA-85-047, vol. 8, no. 47, 11 March 1985.

Lu Li, Independent Federation of Chinese Scholars and Students. Interviewed by Richard W. Marsh, Jr., 30 August 1991.

"Meo Vac Remains Firm in Its War Disposition." *Quan Doi Nhan Dan,* in Joint Publications Research Service, JPRS-SEA-84-086, 12 June 1984.

Minh Nguyen. "Exhibition on Maintenance of Politico-Economic Security and Struggle Against Violators of Socialist Property." *Hanoi Moi,* 19 February 1983, in Joint Publications Research Service, JPRS-SEA-83-412.

Phong Vien. "Trial Reveals Beijing's Black Heart." *Tuan Tin Tuc,* 23 June 1984, in Joint Publications Research Service, JPRS-SEA-84-162, 26 November 1984.

PRC State Education Commission. Directive on policy toward Chinese students and scholars in the United States and Canada. Beijing: transmission to PRC embassies and consulates in the United States and Canada, March 1990.

————. *A Summary of the Meeting of Educational Counselors (Consuls) in Chinese Embassies and Consulates*. Beijing: transmission to PRC embassies and consulates worldwide, March 1990. Translated by the International Federation of Chinese Scholars and Students.

"Secret Paper Describes Myriad Problems in PLA." *Pai Hsing*, in Joint Publications Research Service, JPRS-CAR-91-032, 13 June 1991.

"Security in a Mountain District." *Nhan Dan*, 18 August 1986, in Joint Publications Research Service, JPRS-SEA-86-189, 22 October 1986.

Shanghai City Service. "Shanghai Court Sentences Taiwan Spies." Translated by the Foreign Broadcast Information Service. FBIS daily report—China, regional affairs, FBIS-CHI-90-041, 1 March 1990.

Source no. 1: Former PRC Ministry of Foreign Affairs diplomat who has worked extensively with the MSS and MPS. Interviewed by the author on numerous occasions from 19 March 1991 to 30 September 1992.

Source no. 2: Recruited MSS agent from northern China and a graduate student in the hard sciences in the United States. Interviewed by telephone by the author on several occasions in May 1992.

Source no. 3: Senior member of the International Federation of Chinese Scholars and Students (IFCSS) with firsthand knowledge. Interviewed by Richard W. Marsh, Jr., 20 May 1991.

Source no. 4: Former PRC diplomat to the United States who defected after the Tiananmen Square incident. Interviewed by telephone by the author, 4 September 1992.

Source no. 5: PLA Second Department intelligence officer operating in the United States under illegal cover. Interviewed by telephone by the author (using an interpreter), 23 September 1992.

Source no. 6: Former PLA assistant military attaché who defected to the United States. Interviewed by the author, 16 September 1992.

Source no. 7: Former PLA officer who has served at the military region (MR) and headquarters levels. Interviewed on multiple occasions by Dr. Michael Swaine in August and September 1992.

Source no. 8: PLA intelligence officer who has served as a military diplomat and as an officer at the MR and headquarters levels. Interviewed by the author, 8 November 1992.

Source no. 9: Member of the IFCSS. Interviewed by Richard W. Marsh, Jr., 20 May 1991.

Thanh Binh. "Illegal Fishing Vessels." *Quan Doi Nhan Dan*, 10 November 1985, in Joint Publications Research Service, JPRS-SEA-86-024, 6 February 1986.

Tran Thien Nhien. "From a News Conference to Court Trial." Hanoi Domestic Service, 14 December 1984. Translated by the Foreign Broadcast Information Service. FBIS-APA-84-128, vol. 4, no. 128, 2 July 1984.

Vasilyev, V., Col. "PRC 'Overt Interference' in Afghanistan Hit." *Krasnaya Zvezda,* 23 February 1985, 2d ed. Translated by the Foreign Broadcast Information Service. FBIS-SOV-85-038, vol. 3., no. 38, 26 February 1985.

SECONDARY SOURCES

"Activist Claims Chinese Forced Him to Spy on Democracy Group." *South China Morning Post,* 21 February 1990.

"Aid Worker Who Spoke Out to Learn of Possible Dismissal." *South China Morning Post,* 20 October 1991.

Andrew, Christopher, and Oleg Gordievsky. *Instructions from the Centre: Top-Secret Files on KGB Operations, 1975-1985.* London: Hodder & Stoughton, 1991.

Asia Watch. "Chinese Workers Receive Harsh Sentences." *News from Asia Watch,* 13 March 1991.

―――. "Japan: Harassment of Chinese Dissidents." *News from Asia Watch,* 4 October 1990.

―――. *Punishment Season: Human Rights in China after Martial Law.* New York: Asia Watch Committee, 1990.

Auerbach, Stuart. "President Tells China to Sell Seattle Firm." *Washington Post,* 3 February 1990.

Barnett, A Doak. *Cadres, Bureaucracy, and Political Power in China.* New York: Columbia University Press, 1967.

―――. *The Making of Foreign Policy in China.* Boulder, Colo.: Westview Press, 1985.

Barron, John. *Breaking the Ring: The Bizarre Case of the Walker Family Spy Ring.* Boston: Houghton Mifflin, 1987.

Baum, Julian. "Beijing's Stricter Eye on Foreigners Makes Chinese a Little Wary, Too." *Christian Science Monitor,* 1 May 1987.

Beichman, Arnold. "Wary Eyes on Beijing's Rearmament." *Washington Times,* 20 August 1992.

"Beijing Admits Gathering Information on Residents: Focuses on Anti-Chinese Elements." *South China Morning Post,* 1 April 1992.

Butterfield, Fox. *China: Alive in the Bitter Sea.* New York: Random House, 1990.

————. "China Plans to Let Fewer Students Go Abroad, Especially to the U.S." *New York Times,* 3 September 1989.

————. "Chinese in the U.S.: A Question of Loyalties." *New York Times,* 11 December 1985.

Campbell, Robert. "Sources of Information." Lecture presented at the Federal Law Enforcement Training Center, Glynco, Ga., 15 July 1987.

Central Intelligence Agency. *Directory of Chinese Officials: National-Level Organizations.* CR 85-12068. Washington, D.C.: Government Printing Office, June 1985.

————. *Directory of Chinese Officials and Organizations.* LDA 89-10270. Washington, D.C.: Government Printing Office, 1989.

————. *Military Organizations of the People's Republic of China.* Reference aid, chart, CR 85-15193. Washington, D.C.: Government Printing Office, 1985.

————. *World Factbook 1990.* Washington, D.C.: Government Printing Office, 1990.

Cheung, Tai Ming. "Big Brother Is Watching: China's Internal Security Has Become a Growth Industry." *Far East Economic Review* 142 (3 November 1986): 24–25.

"Chinese Communist Angolan Activity." *Intelligence Digest,* no. 443, October 1975.

"Chinese Reportedly Tried to Get American to Spy." *Washington Post,* 2 November 1988.

Coll, Steve. "Anatomy of a Victory: CIA's Covert Afghan War." *Washington Post,* 19 July 1992.

Deacon, Richard. *The Chinese Secret Service.* London: Grafton Books, 1989.

Defense Intelligence Agency. *Handbook of the Chinese People's Liberation Army.* Washington, D.C.: Defense Intelligence Agency, 1984.

————. *People's Republic of China People's Liberation Army Air Force.* DIC 1300-445-91. Washington, D.C.: Defense Intelligence Agency, 1991.

Dornan, James E., Jr., and Nigel de Lee, eds. *The Chinese War Machine.* London: Salamander Books, 1979.

Du Xichuan and Zhang Lingyuan. *China's Legal System: A General Survey.* Beijing: New World Press, 1990.

Faligot, Roger, and Remi Kauffer. *Kang Shen and the Chinese Secret Service.* New York: William Morrow, 1989.

Findlay, Trever, ed. *Chemical Weapons and Missile Proliferation: With Implications for the Asia/Pacific Region.* Boulder, Colo.: Lynne Reinner Publishers, 1991.

Gertz, Bill. "Chinese Diplomat Denounces Li after Defecting to U.S." *Washington Times,* 7 May 1990.

————. "Sex Is Old Angle in Spying Game." *Washington Times,* 5 May 1987.

Giles, Lionel, trans. *Sun Tzu: The Art of War.* Taipei: Confucius Publishing Co., 1977.

Godwin, Paul. *Development of the Chinese Armed Forces.* Maxwell AFB, Ala.: Air University Press, 1988.

Halloran, Richard. "Secret Is Out on Listing China as Hostile Country." *New York Times,* 25 January 1988.

Hedges, Michael. "Arrest May Affect China's Trade Status." *Washington Times,* 8 May 1990.

Hewitt, Gavin. "The Great Escape from China." *Washington Post,* 2 June 1992.

International Institute for Strategic Studies. *The Military Balance, 1989-1990.* London: Brassey's, 1989.

Jane's Information Group. *China in Crisis: The Role of the Military.* Frome, Somerset: Butler & Tanner, 1989.

Kan, Shirley A. *Chinese Missile and Nuclear Proliferation: Issues for Congress.* Washington, D.C.: Congressional Research Service, 24 August 1992.

Kaufman, Michael T. "New Yorkers Try to Defend Students Hunted in China." *New York Times,* 22 June 1989.

Kent, Sherman. *Strategic Intelligence for American World Policy.* Princeton: Princeton University Press, 1949.

Kierman, Frank A., Jr., and John K. Fairbank, eds. *Chinese Ways in Warfare.* Cambridge: Harvard University Press, 1974.

Knight-Ridder News Service. "Chinese Stole U.S. Neutron Bomb Plans." *Capital* (Annapolis, Md.), 22 November 1990.

Kristof, Nicholas D. "For Chinese Spies, the Enemies are Everywhere." *New York Times,* 18 October 1991.

Lamar, Jacob V. "Spies, Spies Everywhere." *Time,* 9 December 1985.

Law Association for Asia and the Pacific Human Rights Standing Committee. *Defying the Dragon: China and Human Rights in Tibet.* London: Tibet Information Network, 1991.

Lewis, John W., Hua Di, and Xue Litai. "Beijing's Defense Establishment: Solving the Arms-Export Enigma." *International Security* 15 (Spring 1991): 87–109.

Liaowang, in Chinese. Overseas ed., no. 10, 5 March 1990. New York: Synergy Press, 1990.

Lo Ping. "Unstable Regions Set Forth in Top-Secret Document." *Hong Kong Cheng Ming,* no. 171, 1 January 1992.

Lu, Elizabeth. "Spying Admission Stuns Chinese Dissident Group." *Los Angeles Times,* 28 June 1989.

Mecham, Michael. "Bush Overturns Sale to China of Seattle Parts Supply Firm." *Aviation Week and Space Technology,* 12 February 1990.

Oberdorfer, Don. "Chinese Envoy Asks Political Asylum." *Washington Post,* 5 May 1990.

Overend, William. "China Seen Using Close U.S. Ties for Espionage." *Los Angeles Times,* 20 November 1988.

Pear, Robert. "Chinese in U.S. Report Harassment by Beijing." *New York Times,* 27 September 1989.

Praval, Maj. K. C. *The Indian Army after Independence.* New Delhi: Lancer International, 1990.

"PRC Spy Tung Li Sentenced to 12 Years in Taiwan." *United Daily News,* 27 August 1987.

Proceedings of the second annual Staunton Hill Conference on China's People's Liberation Army, Staunton Hill, Va., 6–8 September 1991.

"Resistance Toward Peaceful Evolution." Lecture presented at the annual conference of the Association for Asian Studies, Washington, D.C., 4 April 1992.

"Rhodesia: Kaunda Gives Way." *Intelligence Digest,* no. 413, April 1973.

Richelson, Jeffrey T. *Foreign Intelligence Organizations.* Cambridge: Mass.: Ballinger Publishing Co., 1988.

———. *Sword and Shield: Soviet Intelligence and Security Apparatus.* Cambridge, Mass.: Ballinger Publishing Co., 1986.

Rowland, John. *A History of Sino-Indian Relations: Hostile Co-Existence.* Princeton, N.J.: D. Van Nostrand, 1967.

Rudolph, Jorg-Meinhard. *Cankao Xiaoxi: Foreign News in the Propaganda System of the People's Republic of China.* Baltimore: University of Maryland OPRSCAS, 1984.

Sampson, Catherine. "Peking Keeps Tabs on Foreign 'Spies'." *Times* (London), 8 February 1992.

San Jose Mercury News Service. "Chinese Stole Secret for Neutron Bomb." *Chicago Tribune,* 23 November 1990.

Schlesinger, David. "China Plans Buildup of Spy Network as Communism Wanes." Reuter Newswire, 17 September 1991.

Shenon, Philip. "Two Chinese Depart in Espionage Case." *New York Times,* 31 December 1987.

Simon, Fred, and Merle Goldman, eds. *Science and Technology in Post-Mao China.* Cambridge: Council on East-Asian Studies, Harvard University Press, 1989.

"Society of Military Science Founded." *People's Daily (Renmin Ribao),* in Chinese, 14 January 1991.

Southerland, Daniel. "How China Watches China Watchers." *Washington Post,* 7 September 1986.

Stroud, Heather. "Why I Spoke Out for the Whitehead Refugees." *South China Morning Post,* 28 September 1991.

Sun, Lena H. "Dissident Struggle Still Alive in China." *Washington Post,* 2 June 1991.

———. "Foreign Press Pressed by Chinese System." *Washington Post,* 21 March 1992.

Swaine, Michael. *Military and Political Succession in China: Leadership, Institutions, and Beliefs.* Santa Monica, Calif.: RAND Corp., December 1992.

Tennien, Mark. *No Secret is Safe.* New York: Farrar, Strauss & Young, 1952.

Thorton, Mary. "China Protests U.S. Expulsion of Two Diplomats." *Washington Post,* 1 January 1988.

U.S. Army. Correspondence course of the U.S. Army Intelligence Center and School. Intelligence subcourse 103. *Counterintelligence.* Fort Huchuca, Ariz.: U.S. Army Intelligence Center and School, December 1975.

U.S. Congress. *Immigration Status of Chinese Nationals Currently in the United States.* Washington, D.C.: Government Printing Office, 1989.

U.S. Congress. House. Committee on the Post Office and Civil Service. *Mail Interruption.* 101st Cong., 1st sess., 1989. Serial no. 101-39.

U.S. Congress. House. Foreign Affairs Committee. *Alleged Intimidation and Harassment of Chinese Citizens in the United States.* 41–542. Washington, D.C.: Government Printing Office, June 1990.

U.S. Congress. Joint Economic Committee. *China under the Four Modernizations.* 87–199–0. Washington, D.C.: Government Printing Office, 1981.

U.S. Congress. Office of Technology Assessment. *Technology Transfer to China.* OTA-ISC-340. Washington, D.C.: Government Printing Office, July 1987.

U.S. Congress. Senate. Committee on Governmental Affairs. *The Foreign Missions Act and Espionage Activities in the United States.* 58–439–0. Washington, D.C.: Government Printing Office, 1986.

U.S. Congress. Senate. Select Committee on Intelligence. *Meeting the Espionage Challenge.* 64–268–0. Washington, D.C.: Government Printing Office, 1986.

U.S. Department of Commerce. Bureau of Export Administration. *Action Affecting Export Privileges: Bernardus Johannes Jozef Smit.* Docket no. 9101–01, 22 September 1989.

———. *Denial Orders Currently Affecting Export Privileges.* No. 269, March 1991.

U.S. Department of Justice. Export Control Enforcement Unit, Internal Security Section, Criminal Division. Significant Export Control Cases, January 1981–8 May 1992.

U.S. Department of State. *Diplomatic List, February 1992.* Pub. 7894. Washington, D.C.: Government Printing Office, 1992.

U.S. District Court. United States v. Chin. Vols. 1-6. Criminal docket no. 85–00263–01, 1986.

Van Ness, Peter. *Revolution and Chinese Foreign Policy.* Berkeley and Los Angeles: University of California Press, 1970.

Watkin, Daniel J. "Grand Jury Said to Look at Businessman Linked to Arms-to-China Plot." Associated Press, Newark, N.J., 2 October 1987.

———. "Man Linked to Chinese Diplomats Indicted in Arms Export Conspiracy." Associated Press, Newark, N.J., 8 October 1987.

———. "Plot to Export Missiles to Mainland China Alleged." Associated Press, Newark, N.J., 30 September 1987.

———. "Taiwanese Man Accused in Arms-to-China Case Pleads Guilty." Associated Press, Newark, N.J., 16 December 1987.

Watt, George. *China Spy.* Middlebury, Ind.: Living Sacrifice Books, 1973.

Who's Who in China. Beijing: Foreign Language Press, 1990.

Wills, Morris R., and J. Robert Moskin. *Turncoat: An American's Twelve Years in Communist China.* Englewood Cliffs, N.J.: Prentice-Hall, 1968.

Wise, David, and Thomas B. Ross. *The Espionage Establishment.* New York: Random House, 1967.

"World Politics and Current Affairs." *Economist,* 5 October 1991, 38.

Index

Note: Abbreviations listed in the glossary on pp. XIII-XV are not cross-referenced below. The only three used independently of the organization or activity to which they refer are:

CPC   Chinese Communist Party
PLA   People's Liberation Army
PRC   People's Republic of China

170

About the Author

Nicholas Eftimiades holds a bachelor degree in East Asian Studies from The George Washington University and a masters degree from Joint Military College in Strategic Intelligence. He has lectured on national security and Chinese intelligence at universities, government agencies and testified before Congressional committees.

He has worked in the U.S. Intelligence Community for 15 years, including positions with the CIA, State Department and the Defense Intelligence Agency. He is also an officer in the U. S. Naval Reserve.

In 1993, the National Intelligence Center awarded his monograph, "China's Ministry of State Security: Coming of Age in the International Arena," recognition as the scholarly work of the year on intelligence. This book, Chinese Intelligence Operations, has been published in four languages and is regarded as the first ever scholarly analysis on the subject. He has also made appearances as a featured expert on the CBS Evening News, Dateline NBC, plus other television and radio programs.